Ace the Coding Interview
Must-know Questions

Dr. X.Y. Wang

Contents

1 **Data Structures**   **19**

    1.1   How do you reverse a linked list? 19

    1.2   How do you perform a binary search in a sorted array? 21

    1.3   How can you implement a queue using two stacks? 22

    1.4   Explain how hash tables work. 24

    1.5   How can you traverse a binary tree? 26

    1.6   What is a heap and how is it used? 28

    1.7   Describe how you would implement a graph data structure. 29

    1.8   What is the difference between a stack and a queue? 32

    1.9   How would you detect a cycle in a linked list? . . 34

    1.10   When would you use a tree instead of a hash table? 36

2 Algorithms 39

2.1 Describe how QuickSort works. 39

2.2 Explain the principle of Dynamic Programming. 41

2.3 Can you show me how Breadth-First Search works? 43

2.4 How does the Dijkstra algorithm work? 46

2.5 Can you implement a function to perform a Binary Search? 48

2.6 What is the difference between Merge Sort and Quick Sort? 50

2.7 Explain the Knapsack problem and how you would solve it. 52

2.8 How does the Floyd-Warshall algorithm work? . 55

2.9 How would you find the shortest path in a graph? 57

2.10 How would you find all permutations of a string? 59

3 Time and Space Complexity Analysis 63

3.1 What is Big O notation and why is it important? 63

3.2 Explain the difference between time complexity and space complexity. 65

3.3 How do you determine the time complexity of a recursive function? 67

3.4 What is the time complexity of a hash table insert operation? 69

3.5 What is the time and space complexity of Quick Sort? 70

3.6 Explain how time and space complexity would influence your choice of algorithm. 71

3.7 How does the time complexity of an algorithm affect the performance? 73

3.8 What does O(log n) mean, and can you give an example of an algorithm with this time complexity? 75

3.9 How would you reduce the space complexity of a given algorithm? 78

3.10 What is the worst-case and average-case complexity of a binary search tree? 80

4 Array and String Problems   83

4.1 How would you reverse a string? 83

4.2 Can you find all the permutations of a given string? 85

4.3 How would you check if a string is a palindrome? 86

4.4 How do you find the first non-repeating character in a string? 88

4.5 Can you remove duplicates from a sorted array? 90

4.6   How would you find the missing number in a sequence? 91

4.7   Can you rotate a matrix 90 degrees? 93

4.8   How would you find the maximum subarray sum? 95

4.9   Can you find the longest common prefix in an array of strings? 97

4.10 How would you move all zeros in an array to the end? 98

5   Linked List Problems   101

5.1   How would you reverse a linked list? 101

5.2   Can you find the middle of a linked list? 103

5.3   How would you detect a cycle in a linked list? . . 105

5.4   Can you merge two sorted linked lists? 107

5.5   How would you remove a given node from a linked list? 109

5.6   Can you find the kth to last element of a singly linked list? 111

5.7   How would you partition a linked list around a value x? 112

5.8   Can you add two numbers represented by linked lists? 114

5.9 How would you find the intersection point of two linked lists? 117

5.10 How would you check if a linked list is a palindrome? 119

6 Stack and Queue Problems   123

6.1 Can you design a stack with a function that returns the minimum element in constant time? . . 123

6.2 How would you validate a sequence of pushed and popped elements in a stack? 125

6.3 Can you implement a queue using stacks? 127

6.4 How would you implement a stack using queues? 129

6.5 Can you sort a stack in ascending order (with biggest items on top)? 131

6.6 How would you design a call center with three levels of employees: operator, supervisor, and director using queues? 133

6.7 Can you solve the Tower of Hanoi problem using stacks? 136

6.8 How would you implement a circular queue? . . . 137

6.9 Can you reverse a stack without using any additional data structures? 139

6.10 Can you design a priority queue? 141

7 Tree and Graph Problems   **145**

7.1 How would you determine if a binary tree is bal-
     anced? 145

7.2 Can you implement a Breadth-First Search on a
     graph? 147

7.3 How would you implement a Depth-First Search
     on a graph? 148

7.4 Can you find the lowest common ancestor of two
     nodes in a binary tree? 150

7.5 How would you check if a graph is a tree? 152

7.6 Can you find the shortest path between two nodes
     in a graph? 154

7.7 How would you convert a binary search tree to a
     doubly-linked list? 156

7.8 How would you find the diameter of a binary tree?158

7.9 Can you print the boundary of a binary tree? . . 161

7.10 How would you serialize and deserialize a binary
     tree? 163

8 Recursion and Dynamic Programming Problems165

8.1 Can you write a recursive function to compute
     the Fibonacci sequence? 165

8.2   How would you solve the Tower of Hanoi problem
      using recursion? 167

8.3   How would you implement the coin change prob-
      lem using dynamic programming? 170

8.4   Can you solve the knapsack problem using dy-
      namic programming? 171

8.5   Can you write a recursive function to generate
      all permutations of a string? 173

8.6   How would you solve the problem of climbing
      stairs (you can climb 1 or 2 steps at a time) using
      dynamic programming? 175

8.7   Can you find the longest common subsequence
      of two strings using dynamic programming? . . . 176

8.8   Can you find the number of ways to decode a
      message given a coding scheme using dynamic
      programming? 179

8.9   How would you solve the problem of unique paths
      in a grid using dynamic programming? 180

8.10 Can you implement a function to compute the
      nth number in the Fibonacci sequence using dy-
      namic programming? 182

9 Bit Manipulation Problems   185

9.1   How would you check if a number is a power of
      2 using bit manipulation? 185

9.2 Can you write a function to count the number of bits that are set to 1 in a given number? 187

9.3 How would you swap the values of two integers without using any additional variables? 189

9.4 Can you find the only non-repeating number in an array where every element repeats twice except one, using bit manipulation? 190

9.5 How would you reverse the bits of a given binary number? 192

9.6 Can you find the two non-repeating numbers in an array where every element repeats twice except two, using bit manipulation? 193

9.7 Can you find the maximum of two integers without using if-else or any other comparison operator? 195

9.8 How would you add two numbers without using arithmetic operators? 197

9.9 How would you determine the number of bits required to convert one given integer into another? 199

9.10 Can you find the rightmost set bit in a binary number? 200

10 Understanding System Design   **203**

10.1 Can you describe how you would design a URL shortening service like Bitly? 203

10.2 How would you design a global File Storage Service like Google Drive? 206

10.3 Can you design a web search engine like Google? 209

10.4 How would you design a social network like Facebook? 211

10.5 How would you design a messaging app like WhatsApp? 214

10.6 Can you design an online multiplayer game like Chess? 217

10.7 How would you design a distributed cache? . . . 219

10.8 Can you design a recommendation system like the ones used on Amazon or Netflix? 221

10.9 How would you design a rate limiter for a distributed system? 223

10.10 Can you design a scalable notification service? . . 226

11 Scaling, Data Partitioning, Load Balancing, Caching 229

11.1 How would you horizontally scale a system? . . . 229

11.2 What strategies would you use to partition data? 231

11.3 How would you handle hot spots in your cache? . 234

11.4 Can you describe the different types of load balancers and how they work? 237

11.5 How would you decide between SQL and NoSQL? 239

11.6 How does a CDN work and why is it important? 241

11.7 How would you handle data replication and consistency across multiple databases in different regions? 243

11.8 How does a database index work and why is it important? 246

11.9 How would you implement caching strategies to improve performance? 248

11.10 What are the considerations when choosing between strong and eventual consistency? 250

12 Designing Real-World Systems   253

12.1 Can you design a distributed logging system for a cloud infrastructure? 253

12.2 How would you design a real-time comment system like Reddit or Quora? 256

12.3 How would you design a system to efficiently compute rank on a high frequency basis, like a leaderboard system in games? 258

12.4 Can you design a ride-sharing service like Uber? 261

12.5 How would you design an email delivery system that can ensure email delivery with high availability? 263

12.6 How would you design a service to monitor the uptime of a million websites? 265

12.7 Can you design a hotel reservation system? . . . 268

12.8 How would you design a job scheduler for a distributed system? 270

12.9 How would you design a distributed lock for a distributed system? 273

12.10 Can you design a garbage collection system? . . . 275

Preface

I am thrilled to welcome you to "Ace the Coding Interview: Must-know Questions." If you've found yourself holding this book, it likely means that you are at the threshold of embarking on one of the most exciting and challenging phases of your career journey - the technical interview. This critical stage can be a make-or-break point for many aspiring software developers, engineers, and IT professionals. This book has been meticulously designed as a comprehensive guide to navigate these challenges with confidence and command.

The field of computer science is fascinating, complex, and ever-evolving. To thrive in it, one must have a deep understanding of its various elements, such as data structures, algorithms, complexity analysis, along with practical problem-solving skills. However, mastering these areas alone is often not enough. Conveying your knowledge in an interview setting, under pressure, is a different ball game altogether. That's where this book comes into play.

In "Ace the Coding Interview," we delve into the core of these fundamental concepts, breaking them down for easy understanding while also demonstrating their practical application.

The aim is not just to facilitate rote learning, but to foster a deep and intuitive understanding of the principles involved. Each chapter is composed of a plethora of carefully curated questions that are frequently asked during technical interviews. These questions range from essential basic concepts to more intricate problems requiring creative problem-solving skills. Solutions to these problems are explained in a detailed yet concise manner to enable you to think analytically and problem-solve efficiently.

One of the unique features of this book is the segment on system design and real-world applications. As you progress in your career, the ability to design scalable systems and understand real-world applications of your code becomes equally, if not more, important. This book gives you an insight into that world, preparing you for the advanced stages of your career.

Another important aspect that sets this book apart is the last segment, which focuses on scaling, data partitioning, load balancing, and caching. With the rise of distributed systems and cloud computing, these topics have become essential knowledge for any software engineer.

"Ace the Coding Interview" serves not only as an interview preparation resource but also as a handy reference guide for your professional journey. It is my hope that this book demystifies the process of technical interviews and equips you with the confidence, knowledge, and problem-solving skills required to excel in them.

Remember, the ultimate goal is not just to secure the job offer but to grow and thrive as a skilled, insightful, and innovative professional in the world of computer science. This journey is one of continuous learning and improvement, and this book is here to assist you at every step of the way.

Enjoy the journey, and here's to your success!

Chapter 1

Data Structures

1.1 How do you reverse a linked list?

Reversing a linked list is a common operation in data structures and is often asked in coding interviews. Let's discuss the iterative method to reverse a linked list first.

Here is the algorithm:

1. Initialize three pointers 'prev' as NULL, 'curr' as head and 'next' as NULL.

2. Iterate through the linked list. In the loop, do following:

- (a) Before changing 'next' of 'curr', store next node using 'next = curr->next'

- (b) Now change next of current, set 'curr->next' to 'prev' (this is the actual reversing process)

- (c) Move 'prev' and 'curr' one step forward

3. Return prev (it will become new head).

Assuming 'ListNode' is your data structure for a list node, the code in C++ would be:

```cpp
ListNode* reverse(ListNode* head) {
    ListNode* prev = NULL;
    ListNode* curr = head;
    while (curr != NULL) {
        ListNode* nextTemp = curr->next;
        curr->next = prev;
        prev = curr;
        curr = nextTemp;
    }
    return prev;
}
```

This function reverses the linked list by iterating over the list and rearranging the 'next' pointer of each node.

You can also solve this problem using recursion. The idea is to reverse the rest of the list first, then take the first node and attach it to the end of reversed list. The base case is when 'head' is 'NULL'.

Here's the Python recursive solution:

```python
def reverse(self, head):
    if head is None or head.next is None:
        return head
    else:
        newHead = self.reverse(head.next)
        head.next.next = head
        head.next = None
    return newHead
```

'head.next.next = head' makes the next node of head point to itself, in essence taking the first node and putting it at the end of the reversed list, 'head.next = None' then severs the link between the first node and the rest of the list.

In this code, 'newHead' is the pointer to the new head of the reversed list.

1.2   How do you perform a binary search in a sorted array?

Binary search is one of the fastest searching algorithms, with a time complexity of O(log n). It works by repeatedly dividing the search interval in half. The algorithm works only on sorted arrays.

Here's a step by step guide on how it's implemented:

1. Find the middle element of the array. If the array has an even number of elements, the middle element is calculated as 'mid = low + (high - low) / 2' where high is the index of the last element and low is the index of the first element (often 0). This method is more effective than '(low + high) / 2' as it avoids integer overflow for large values of low and high.

2. Compare the middle element with the target value. If the target value matches the middle element, return the middle index.

3. If the target value is less than the middle element, repeat the search with the left half of the array.

4. If the target value is greater than the middle element, repeat the search with the right half of the array.

5. Repeat step 1 to 4 until the target value is found or the search interval is empty.

Here is a Python example code for binary search:

```
def binary_search(array, target):
    low = 0
    high = len(array) - 1

    while low <= high:
        mid = low + (high - low) // 2

        if array[mid] == target:
            return mid
        elif array[mid] < target:
            low = mid + 1
        else:
            high = mid - 1

    return -1 # Element is not present in the array
```

For instance, if you have a sorted array of '[1, 3, 5, 7, 9]' and you're searching for '3', the function 'binary_search([1, 3, 5, 7, 9], 3)' will return '1' which is the index of '3' in the given array.

Please note, the binary search algorithm is a divide and conquer algorithm, in each step, it reduces the search space by half. As a result, the time complexity of binary search is logarithmic.

1.3   How can you implement a queue using two stacks?

Queue is a First In First Out (FIFO) data structure whereas Stack is a Last In First Out (LIFO) data structure. However, we can implement a Queue using two Stacks.

Here's how:

- Let's say we have two stacks: $S1$ and $S2$.

- Enqueue operation (insert operation) is implemented using the $S1$ stack.

- When performing a Dequeue operation (delete operation), if the $S2$ stack is empty, pop all elements from $S1$ and push them to $S2$. Then pop the top element from $S2$.

- If the $S2$ stack is not empty during the Dequeue operation, simply pop the top element from the $S2$ stack.

Below is a Python implementation of the aforementioned:

```python
class Queue:
    def __init__(self):
        self.s1 = []
        self.s2 = []

    def enqueue(self, item):
        self.s1.append(item)

    def dequeue(self):
        if not self.s2:
            while self.s1:
                self.s2.append(self.s1.pop())
        return self.s2.pop()
```

To explain the above code:

- Enqueue operation: A new element is always added to $S1$ stack.

- Dequeue operation: If $S2$ is not empty then the top of the stack is returned, else all the elements from $S1$ are moved to $S2$ and finally top of $S2$ is returned.

The complexity of the enqueue operation (i.e., adding an item) is $O(1)$, and dequeue operation varies:

- If $S2$ already contains elements, the complexity is $O(1)$.

- If $S2$ is empty, we have to transfer n elements from $S1$ to $S2$, which gives a complexity of $O(n)$.

However, in Amortized Complexity analysis, which is the total time taken for n operations or the average time per operation, the dequeue operation is $O(1)$. This is because for n insertions there will be n deletions. Therefore, every element is transferred from $S1$ to $S2$ only 2 times. Hence the amortized complexity is $O(1)$.

1.4   Explain how hash tables work.

Hash tables are a type of data structure that allow for fast data retrieval and storage. They allow a program to access a data value given a key, in constant time O(1), on average.

Here's how they work:

1. Hash Function:

A hash table utilizes a hash function that takes an input (or 'key') and returns an index into an array where the corresponding value is stored. The hash function is used to convert the key into a unique index (hash code), which is used to find the desired value.

Suppose our hash function is 'h(k) = k mod 10', where 'k mod 10' is the remainder when 'k' is divided by 10.

If we want to store a value with the key 23, our hash function would compute 'h(23) = 23 mod 10 = 3'. So, we store the corresponding value at the index 3 in our hash table.

2. Handling Collisions:

Collisions occur when the hash function returns the same index for two different keys. There two main methods to handle collisions: separate chaining and open addressing.

- Separate Chaining: Each index in the array points to a linked list. When a collision occurs, the new key-value pair is added to the end of the linked list at the relevant index.

- Open Addressing: When a collision occurs, we find the next available slot in the array and use that to store our new key-value pair.

3. Load Factor and Resizing:

The load factor is a measure that determines when to increase the size of the hash table. It is calculated as the ratio of the number of elements to the size of the array.

If we have a hash table of size 10 and 8 elements stored in it, then 'load factor = $8/10 = 0.8$'. When the load factor surpasses a certain threshold (typically 0.7), the hash table is resized.

The following pseudocode illustrates a simple hash table using an array:

```
class HashTable
    initialize(size):
        data = new Array(size)

    __hash(key):
        hash = 0
        for(let i = 0; i < key.length; i++):
            hash = (hash + key.charCodeAt(i) * i) % data.length
        return hash

    insert(key, value):
        address = this.__hash(key)
        if(!data[address]):
            data[address] = []
        data[address].push([key, value])
        return address

    lookup(key):
        address = this.__hash(key)
        if(data[address]):
            for(let i = 0; i < data[address].length; i++)
                if(data[address][i][0] == key)
```

```
            return data[address][i][1]
    return null
```

In this code, '___hash()' is a simple hash function that converts the key to an index in the data array. The 'insert()' method hashes the key and push a new array containing the key and value to the hashed address. The 'lookup()' function also hashes the key but then tries to find it in the data array. If it finds it, it returns the value, else it returns null.

1.5   How can you traverse a binary tree?

Traversing a Binary Tree means visiting every node in the tree. There are several ways to do this, typically divided into two approaches: Depth First and Breadth First.

1. Depth First Search (DFS): This approach prioritizes going as deep into the tree as possible. There are three forms of DFS.

- **In-order Traversal**: With this approach, you first visit the left subtree, then the current node, and finally, the right subtree. If we denote nodes by '(L, N, R)' standing for (Left child, Node, Right child), in-order traversal follows the 'L-N-R' pattern.

- **Pre-order Traversal**: With this approach, you first visit the current node, then the left subtree, and finally, the right subtree. It follows the 'N-L-R' pattern.

- **Post-order Traversal**: With this approach, you first visit the left subtree, then the right subtree, and finally, the current node. It follows the 'L-R-N' pattern.

Here is a Python code example of these traversals for a binary tree.

```
class Node:
    def __init__(self, key):
        self.left = None
        self.right = None
        self.val = key

def printInorder(root):
    if root:
        printInorder(root.left)
        print(root.val),
        printInorder(root.right)

def printPostorder(root):
    if root:
        printPostorder(root.left)
        printPostorder(root.right)
        print(root.val),

def printPreorder(root):
    if root:
        print(root.val),
        printPreorder(root.left)
        printPreorder(root.right)
```

2. Breadth First Search (BFS): This approach travels the tree level by level. This is also known as level-order traversal.

A common BFS algorithm is the level-order traversal. It visits each node in level order from left to right. This traversal uses a queue to hold nodes to visit next.

Here is a Python code example of level-order traversal.

```
from collections import deque

class Node:
    def __init__(self, key):
        self.left = None
        self.right = None
        self.val = key

def printLevelOrder(root):
    if not root:
        return

    queue = deque()
    queue.append(root)

    while queue:
        node = queue.popleft()
```

```
print(node.val),

if node.left:
    queue.append(node.left)
if node.right:
    queue.append(node.right)
```

Both DFS and BFS have their uses: DFS is helpful for queries such as "Is there a path to X?", while BFS can answer questions like "What is the shortest (or longest) path to X?".

1.6   What is a heap and how is it used?

A heap is a specialized tree-based data structure in computer science that satisfies the heap property. This is an abstract data type that can be visualized as a binary tree.

In a heap data structure, the heap property is primarily of two types:

- **Max-Heap**: In a max-heap, for any given node I, the value of I is greater than or equal to the values of its children.

$$\text{Parent node value} \geq \text{Child node values}$$

- **Min-Heap**: In a min-heap, for any given node I, the value of I is less than or equal to the values of its children.

$$\text{Parent node value} \leq \text{Child node values}$$

Heap data structures are mainly used to implement priority queues (efficiently finding or accessing the maximum OR min-

imum element of a queue), where elements with higher importance are prioritized before elements with lower importance. It
has a wide range of applications such as load balancing, scheduling tasks in operating systems or in algorithms such as Heap-
sort and Dijkstra's algorithm for finding the shortest path in a
graph.

In the max-heap shown above, for any given node i.. the value
of i is larger than or equal to the values of its children. It's the
opposite in a min-heap.

Here are some important operations in a binary heap and their
time complexities:

- **insert**: Insert a new key. (O(logN))

- **getMax or getMin**: Returns the root. (O(1))

- **extractMax or extractMin**: Removes and returns the root.
(O(logN))

- **deleteKey**: Deletes a key from the heap. (O(logN))

1.7 Describe how you would implement a graph data structure.

A graph data structure consists of a collection of nodes (also
called vertices) and a collection of edges. Each edge connects
a pair of nodes. Graphs may be either directed (edges have a
direction) or undirected.

There are different ways you can implement a graph in code,
each with their relative strengths and weaknesses. The two
most common implementations are an adjacency matrix and

an adjacency list. I will describe how to implement both of
these.

1. Adjacency Matrix

In an adjacency matrix implementation, the graph is represented by a matrix (usually a 2D array in code) where the cell
at the i-th row and j-th column (denoted as M[i][j]) is true (or
1) if there's an edge from node i to node j, or false (or 0) otherwise. This works for both directed and undirected graphs. If
the graph is undirected, the matrix will be symmetric around
the diagonal.

```
class Graph:
    def __init__(self, num_of_vertices):
        self.num_of_vertices = num_of_vertices
        self.adjMatrix = [[0]*num_of_vertices for i in range(
            num_of_vertices)]
```

The adjacency matrix representation is suitable when the graph
is dense, i.e., the number of edges is close to the maximum
possible number of edges. Its time complexity for checking the
existence of an edge is constant, i.e., $O(1)$.

However, it's poor in terms of space complexity, i.e., $O(V^2)$,
where V is the number of vertices.

2. Adjacency List

In an adjacency list implementation, the graph is represented
by a map from nodes to lists of nodes (usually array of lists or
linked lists):

```
class Graph:
    def __init__(self, num_of_vertices):
        self.num_of_vertices = num_of_vertices
        self.adjList = [[] for i in range(num_of_vertices)]

    def add_edge(self, src, dest):
```

```
self.adjList[src].append(dest)
self.adjList[dest].append(src) # For undirected graph
```

Each node i is associated with a list that contains the nodes to which i has an edge. The adjacency list representation is suitable when the graph is sparse, i.e., the number of edges is far less than the maximum possible number of edges.

Its time complexity for checking the existence of an edge is linear in the degree of the node, i.e., $O(d)$, where d is the degree of a node. However, it's efficient in terms of space complexity, i.e., $O(V + E)$, where V is the number of vertices and E is the number of edges.

For example, if a graph data structure has five vertices and four edges in an undirected graph:

```
0 -- 1
|    |
3 -- 2 -- 4
```

The adjacency matrix and adjacency list representations will be:

For adjacency matrix:

```
   0 1 2 3 4
0[0 1 0 1 0]
1[1 0 1 0 0]
2[0 1 0 1 1]
3[1 0 1 0 0]
4[0 0 1 0 0]
```

For adjacency list:

```
0: 1, 3
1: 0, 2
2: 1, 3, 4
3: 0, 2
4: 2
```

In summary, choose the type of representation based on the expected graph's density to achieve the best trade-off between time and space complexities.

1.8   What is the difference between a stack and a queue?

Both stacks and queues are abstract data types that can store items in an order. However, the principal or the basic differences between them are the order of elements and their operations: addition (push/enqueue) and removal (pop/dequeue).

Stack: A stack is a linear data structure which follows a particular order in which the operations are performed. The order may be Last In First Out (LIFO) or First In Last Out (FILO).

The main operations associated with stack are:

- Push: Adds an element to the stack. If the stack is full, it results in an Overflow condition.

- Pop: Removes an element from the stack. The items are popped in the reverse order in which they are pushed. If the stack is empty, it results in an Underflow condition.

Here's a mathematical notion of a stack with *push* and *pop* operations. Let s be a stack and x be an element, then:

1. $push(s, x)$ inserts x at the top of stack s.

2. $pop(s)$ removes the top most element from the stack s.

There are many real-life examples of a stack. Consider a stack of plates, where the plate at the top is the first one to be removed, i.e., the plate that was pushed last is popped first.

Queue: A queue is a linear data structure that stores elements in a sequential manner, following a First-In-First-Out (FIFO) rule. This means that the item that is added (enqueued) first, is the first one to be removed (dequeued).

The primary operations associated with queue are:

- Enqueue: Adds an element to the end of the queue.

- Dequeue: Removes an element from the front of the queue.

Here's a mathematical notion of a queue with *enqueue* and *dequeue* operations. Let q be a queue and x be an element, then:

1. $enqueue(q, x)$ adds x at the end of queue q.

2. $dequeue(q)$ removes the first element from the queue q.

As an example, the queue in a supermarket is the best example of a queue, where the person who comes first is served first (the person is removed from the queue).

In summary, the primary distinguishing characteristic of stacks and queues are their rules for element access (item removal): stacks are LIFO/FILO while queues are FIFO.

1.9 How would you detect a cycle in a linked list?

Detecting a cycle in a linked list is a common interview problem in computer science and it tests your knowledge on the data structure, especially linked lists, and algorithms.

Here are a couple of ways you can do this:

1. Hashing Method

The simplest way to detect a cycle in a linked list is by using a hash table. This method involves traversing the linked list one node at a time. For every node, check if it is in the hash table. If it is, then there is a cycle present. If the node is not in the hash table, add it and move to the next node.

```
Let us write the pseudo-code:

Initialize an empty hash table

For each node in the linked list:
    if the node is not in the hash table:
        add the node to the hash table
    else:
        return True // cycle detected

return False // cycle not detected
```

However, this method may not be efficient in terms of space complexity (in worst case, $O(n)$ where n is the number of nodes).

2. Floyd's Cycle Finding Algorithm (Two Pointers Method)

The second, more optimized solution involves using two pointers that traverse the list at different speeds (typically called 'slow' and 'fast' pointers). The 'slow' pointer moves one node at a time while the 'fast' pointer moves two nodes. If there is a cycle in the list, the 'fast' pointer will end up looping around and meeting the 'slow' pointer again. If there is no cycle, the 'fast' pointer will reach the end of the list.

```
Let us write the pseudo-code:

Initialize slow pointer to head of the list
Initialize fast pointer to head of the list

While fast pointer is not null and fast.next is not null:
  Move slow pointer one step
  Move fast pointer two steps

  if slow pointer is equal to fast pointer:
    return True   // cycle detected

return False   // cycle not detected
```

In this method, no additional space is required, hence the space complexity is constant $O(1)$. This algorithm is also known as the "hare and tortoise" algorithm, because of the different speeds at which the pointers traverse the list.

Mathematical Representation

For Floyd's cycle finding algorithm, if we assume there is a cycle, and denote the distance from the head to the cycle start as 'x', the cycle length as 'y', and the distance from the cycle start to the meeting point of 'slow' and 'fast' as 'z'.

When 'slow' and 'fast' meet, we have:

distance traveled by slow $= x + z$

distance traveled by fast $= x + z + n \cdot y$ (n is the number of laps 'fast' has taken in the cycle)

Since 'fast' travels at twice the speed of 'slow', we get:

$2 \cdot (x + z) = x + z + n \cdot y$

Solving this, we get

$$x = (n - 1) \cdot y + (y - z)$$

which means:

- the distance from the head of the list to the start of the cycle is equal to

- the number of complete cycle rounds the fast pointer has made minus 1 times the cycle length plus

- the cycle length minus the distance of the meeting point from the start of the cycle.

If we start two pointers again from the meeting point and the head, they will meet at the start of the cycle since the distances they have to travel are exactly the same. This can be used to find the starting point of the cycle.

Both these algorithms are useful ways to detect cycles in linked lists, and the approach you choose can depend on the specific requirements of your problem, such as whether you have space limitations.

Please note that these solutions work mainly for singly-linked lists. For doubly-linked lists, we could take advantage of the backward link to solve the problem using different approaches.

1.10   When would you use a tree instead of a hash table?

There are several scenarios where a tree is more advantageous than a hash table.

1. **Ordered Data**: Trees are commonly used with an ordering criterion. They allow relatively efficient insertions, deletions and lookups, which makes them suitable for situations where order matters. A tree-based data structure like a Binary Search Tree (BST) keeps its elements sorted in order, which facilitates operations like searching for an element in the tree: the average time complexity is O(log n). In contrast, while hash tables provide efficient searching capabilities, they do not maintain any order.

2. **Range Queries**: If an application involves a lot of range queries (e.g., find all numbers between x and y), trees are a better choice. This operation is extremely inefficient in a hash table. For example, you can do an in-order traversal of a BST pretty efficiently.

3. **Min/Max Lookup:** Tree structures like a Binary Heap can be used efficiently to model a priority queue, which provides quick operations to look for, insert, or delete from a collection of items based on priority. With a binary heap, you can find the min/max element in constant O(1) time. While hash tables offer efficient lookup, insert and delete operations, they do not provide a quick way to identify the minimum or maximum values.

4. **Duplicated Keys:** Trees can handle the duplication of keys efficiently. Suppose we talk about the BST, if you try to insert a duplicated key, it would go as left child (or right depending upon the rules you are following). In hash tables, duplicate keys aren't allowed by default.

These are broad guidelines and the choice of data structure would depend on a variety of factors such as the nature of the problem, the specific requirements of the operation, and the characteristics of the input data.

Here's an example of a Binary Search Tree:

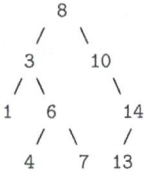

```
      8
    /   \
   3     10
  / \      \
 1   6      14
    / \    /
   4   7 13
```

In this BST tree, the left subtree of a node contains only nodes
with keys less than the node's key. The right subtree of a node
contains only nodes with keys greater than the node's key.

Chapter 2

Algorithms

2.1 Describe how QuickSort works.

Quicksort is a widely used sorting algorithm that, on average, makes O(n log n) comparisons to sort n items. It is a comparison sort and, in efficient implementations, is not a stable sort. Quicksort can operate in-place on an array, requiring small additional amounts of memory to perform the sorting.

The basic idea behind quicksort is to:

1. Choose a "pivot" element from the array and partition the other elements into two sub-arrays, according to whether they are less than or greater than the pivot. The pivot element is then in its final position.

2. This is done recursively, where we sort the sub-arrays in a similar manner, until the base case is reached (arrays of size zero or one are already sorted).

The steps to implement QuickSort are as follows:

1. Choose an element in the array as the pivot. The choice of pivot can vary - it could be the first element, the last element, a random element, or the median. Different pivot-picking strategies can affect the complexity.

2. Partition the array into two segments. In the first segment, all elements are less than or equal to the pivot and in the second segment, all elements are greater than the pivot. This step is the key to QuickSort and is performed using a method called "Partitioning".

3. Recursively implement QuickSort on the two segments.

The pseudo-code implementation of quicksort is:

```
function quicksort(array)
   if length(array) <= 1
      return array
   select and remove a pivot value 'pivot' from array
   create empty lists 'less' and 'greater'
   for each x in array
      if x <= pivot then append x to 'less'
      else append x to 'greater'
   return concatenate(quicksort(less), pivot, quicksort(greater))
```

The partition step is very crucial and can be done in the following way:

```
function partition(array, low, high)
   pivot = array[high]
   i = (low - 1)
   for j = low to high-1
      if array[j] < pivot
         i++
         swap array[i] and array[j]
   swap array[i + 1] and array[high]
   return (i + 1)
```

In mathematical notation, the worst-case time complexity of QuickSort is $O(n^2)$ and the best-case and average-case time complexity is O(n log n), where n is the number of elements in the array to be sorted. In practice, QuickSort often outperforms other sorting algorithms for larger datasets.

2.2 Explain the principle of Dynamic Programming.

Dynamic Programming (DP) is a powerful method in computer science for solving optimization problems, counting problems, and combinatorial problems. It's a technique to solve problems by breaking them down into smaller subproblems. The solutions to these subproblems are then combined to solve the original problem, and thus allowing us to arrive at the desired solution more efficiently. In a way, it's a kind of divide-and-conquer approach. However, what makes DP unique and more optimized is that it stores the solutions to subproblems to avoid re-computing them, which is also known as memoization.

The idea behind dynamic programming is mainly based on the following two entities:

1. **Bellman's Principle of Optimality**: This principle states that an optimal policy (solution) has the property that whatever the initial state and initial decision are, the remaining decisions must constitute an optimal policy (solution) with regard to the state resulting from the initial decision.

2. **Overlapping Subproblems Property**: This property is the cornerstone of Dynamic Programming. A problem is said to have overlapping subproblems if the problem can be broken down into subproblems which are reused several times or a recursive algorithm for the problem solves the same subproblem

over and over rather than always generating new subproblems. In simpler terms, if a recursive problem can be solved by solving smaller instances of identical problems, then we can use the DP technique.

The main process of Dynamic Programming can be broken down in the following steps:

1. **Step 1 (Analyzing subproblems)**: Break the problem down into smaller subproblems. These subproblems are not independent. In fact, the solution to one subproblem may depend on the solutions to various others.

2. **Step 2 (Memoization or "Remember your results")**: Once a subproblem has been solved, its solution is stored in a table so that it can be directly retrieved if needed again, thus avoiding re-computing the solution.

3. **Step 3 (Constructing an optimal solution to the problem)**: Using the solutions to the subproblems, solve the original problem.

A simple example of Dynamic Programming is the calculation of Fibonacci series where overlapping subproblems occur. Here, each number in the series is the sum of two preceding ones.

```
def Fibonacci(n):
    if n<=0:
        print("Incorrect input")
    elif n==1:
        return 0
    elif n==2:
        return 1
    else:
        return Fibonacci(n-1) + Fibonacci(n-2)
```

Without dynamic programming, as the recursion depth increases, we solve the same subproblems repeatedly. To overcome this

and increase efficiency, we save the result of each subproblem
so we don't need to compute it each time it's needed.

```
def Fibonacci(n):
    fibArray = [0,1]
    while len(fibArray) < n+1:
        fibArray.append(0)

    if n<=1:
        return n
    else:
        if fibArray[n-1] == 0:
            fibArray[n-1] = Fibonacci(n-1)
        if fibArray[n-2] == 0:
            fibArray[n-2] = Fibonacci(n-2)

        fibArray[n] = fibArray[n-2] + fibArray[n-1]
    return fibArray[n]
```

There's no concrete DP formula, as its implementation very
much depends on the problem at hand. Typically, the DP solution is based on a recurrence relation and the initial terms of
the relation are solved in a bottom-up manner.

2.3   Can you show me how Breadth-First Search works?

Breadth-First Search or BFS is an algorithm for traversing or
searching tree or graph data structures. Given a graph and a
source vertex in the graph, BFS explores the neighbor vertices
at the present depth prior to moving on to vertices at the next
depth level.

Here is a more detailed explanation about how BFS works:

Breadth-First Search (BFS) starts traversal from the root node
and visits nodes in a level by level manner (i.e., visiting the

ones nearest to the root first). It uses a queue data structure
to keep track of nodes yet to be explored.

1. Queue up the start node (root) and mark it as visited.

2. While there are nodes in the queue:

  1. Dequeue the next node.

  2. If this node is the goal (destination), then finish.

  3. Otherwise, enqueue any neighbour nodes that haven't been visited yet, and mark them as visited.

Here's an example of BFS using the following undirected graph,
starting from node/vertex A:

```
  B --- D
 /      | \
A ----  C   E
```

Queue: [A]

1. Visit A (Dequeue A and Enqueue its neighbours B and C
into Queue)

Queue: [B, C]

2. Visit B (Dequeue B and Enqueue D (A is already visited)
into Queue)

Queue: [C, D]

3. Visit C (Dequeue C and Enqueue None as node C does not
have any unvisited neighbours)

Queue: [D]

4. Visit D (Dequeue D and Enqueue E (B and A are already visited) into Queue)

Queue: [E]

5. Visit E (Dequeue E and Enqueue None as it doesn't have any unvisited neighbors).

Queue: []

Traversal Sequence: A B C D E

Just to clarify, this is just one of the possible traversal sequences because BFS can lead to different results when the nodes are enqueued in different orders, but all sequences will have nodes in the same levels grouped together.

In terms of time complexity, BFS has a time complexity of $O(V+E)$, where V is the number of vertices and E is the number of edges, as every vertex and every edge will be explored in the worst case.

Pseudocode for BFS:

'

```python
BFS(graph, root):
    create empty set visited and queue Q
    add root to visited and enqueue it into Q
    while Q is not empty do
        v = dequeue(Q)
        for each edge e = (v, w) in graph.adjacentEdges(v) do
            if w not in visited do
                add w to visited
                enqueue w into Q
```

2.4   How does the Dijkstra algorithm work?

Dijkstra's algorithm is a popular method used to find the shortest path between two nodes in a graph. Here is a general step-by-step procedure on how this algorithm works:

1. Initialization: Start at the node at which you are starting (call it the initial node). Set its 'distance' to zero and set the 'distance' for all other nodes to infinity.

2. Examine unvisited nodes: Visit all the unvisited neighbors of the current node. Calculate their tentative distance from the starting point through the current node. Compare the newly calculated tentative distance with the current assigned value and assign the smaller one.

3. Mark node as visited: After considering all of the unvisited neighbors of the current node, mark the current node as 'visited'. Visited nodes are not checked again.

4. Select next node: Out of the unvisited nodes, choose the node with the smallest tentative distance (priority queue can be used for this), set that as the current node, and go back to step 2.

5. Stop: If the destination node has been marked as visited (when planning a route between two specific nodes) or if the smallest tentative distance among the nodes in the unvisited set is infinity (no connection between initial and remaining unvisited nodes), stop the algorithm.

In mathematical terms:

Let $G = (V, E)$ with non-negative edge weights $w : E \rightarrow R$.

Let $d(v)$ denote the length of a shortest path from a vertex s to vertex v.

The Dijkstra's Algorithm operates as follows:

1. **Initialization:**

s is the source vertex. Distances to all vertices are set to

+

$$d(s) = 0$$

+

$$d(v) = \infty$$

for all vs

2. All vertices are marked as unvisited and are inserted into a priority queue

3. Until the queue is empty, a vertex u with the smallest distance value is selected from the queue and its unvisited adjacent vertices are relaxed as follows:

+

$$if\ d(u) + w(u,v) < d(v)$$

+

$$then\ d(v)\ is\ updated\ to\ d(u) + w(u,v)$$

+ and new parent of v is set to u.

+ Then, u is marked as visited.

4. The algorithm concludes when the queue is empty.

Dijkstra's algorithm typically uses a priority queue to select the vertex with minimum distance more quickly. It's the basis of many routing protocols in modern systems, whether finding

the optimal route between two locations on a map or routing
packets over the internet.

Note that Dijkstra's algorithm assumes that all edge weights
are non-negative, as it greedily selects the smallest edge at each
step.

2.5   Can you implement a function to perform a Binary Search?

Binary search is a fast search algorithm with a runtime complexity of O(log n). A binary search works by comparing an
input value to the middle element of a sorted array. Depending
on whether the input is less than or greater than the middle
element, the algorithm "narrows down" the search to the lower
or upper half of the array and repeats the process.

Here's a simple implementation of binary search in Python:

```python
def binary_search(arr, low, high, x):
    if high >= low:
        mid = (high + low) // 2
        if arr[mid] == x:
            return mid
        elif arr[mid] > x:
            return binary_search(arr, low, mid - 1, x)
        else:
            return binary_search(arr, mid + 1, high, x)
    else:
        return -1
```

Here's how this implementation works:

- The function "binary_search" takes four arguments: a sorted
array "arr", the lowest index "low", the highest index "high",
and the value "x" that we're searching for.

- If 'high' is greater than or equal to 'low', it calculates the value of 'mid' as the floor division of the sum of 'high' and 'low'. This value indicates the index of the middle element of the current array slice.

- It then compares the middle element of the array (i.e., 'arr[mid]') to 'x'. If they're equal, it returns the index 'mid'.

- If 'arr[mid]' is greater than 'x', it performs a binary search on the left half of the array (i.e., from index 'low' to 'mid-1') and returns the result.

- If 'arr[mid]' is less than 'x', it performs a binary search on the right half of the array (i.e., from index 'mid+1' to 'high') and returns the result.

- If 'high' is less than 'low', it means that 'x' is not present in the array, so the function returns '-1'.

Here's how you can call this function:

```
arr = [2, 3, 4, 10, 40]
x = 10
result = binary_search(arr, 0, len(arr)-1, x)
if result != -1:
    print('Element is present at index', str(result))
else:
    print('Element is not present in array')
```

This code defines a sorted array 'arr' and a value 'x' to search for in the array. It then calls 'binary_search', passing the array, the first and last index of the array, and the value to search for. If 'binary_search' returns something other than '-1', the code prints the index at which 'x' is found in the array. If 'binary_search' returns '-1', it prints a message indicating that 'x' is not present in the array.

2.6   What is the difference between Merge Sort and Quick Sort?

Merge Sort and Quick Sort are both effective sorting algorithms with distinctive approaches, and each has its strengths and weaknesses. The main differences between Merge Sort and Quick Sort can be summarized in five points:

1. **Divide and Conquer Strategy**: Both algorithms use a divide and conquer strategy, but they apply it differently.

- Merge Sort divides the unsorted list into N sublists, each comprising one element (a list of one element is considered sorted), and then repeatedly merges the sublists to produce new sorted sublists until there is only one sublist remaining.

- Quick Sort, on the other hand, selects a 'pivot' element from the array and partitions the other elements into two sub-arrays, according to whether they are less than or greater than the pivot. The pivot is then positioned in its proper place in the sorted array, and the process repeats for the sub-arrays on either side of the pivot.

2. **Worst-Case and Average Time Complexity**:

Merge sort performs evenly in all cases (best, average, and worst) with a time complexity of O(n log n). Quick Sort performs very well on average, with a time complexity of O(n log n), but has a worst-case scenario of $O(n^2)$, which can happen when the pivot elements are not chosen optimally, for example, in a sorted or reverse sorted array.

3. **Space Complexity**:

Merge sort requires more space, with a space complexity of O(n), as it uses auxiliary space for the temporary arrays during the merge process, while Quick Sort doesn't require any extra space and has a space complexity of O(log n) because it sorts the elements in place.

4. **Stability**:

Merge sort is a stable sorting algorithm, meaning that equal elements maintain their relative order after sorting is performed. Conversely, Quick Sort is not inherently stable, but it can be made stable with some modifications.

5. **Usage Scenarios**:

Merge sort is often preferred for sorting linked lists because of efficient operations, high stability, and better cases when sufficient auxiliary space is present. Quick Sort is typically preferred for arrays due to in-place sorting, less space usage, and excellent average case time complexity.

Here is the pseudocode of both sorting algorithms to illustrate the approach:

1. **Merge Sort**:

```
MergeSort(arr[], l, r)
If r > l
1. Find middle point to divide the array into two halves:
    middle m = l+ (r-l)/2
2. Call mergeSort for first half:
    Call mergeSort(arr, l, m)
3. Call mergeSort for second half:
    Call mergeSort(arr, m+1, r)
4. Merge the two halves sorted in step 2 and 3:
    Call merge(arr, l, m, r)
```

2. **Quick Sort**:

```
QuickSort(arr[], low, high)
If (low < high)
1. pi is partitioning index, arr[pi] is now
   at right place
   pi = partition(arr, low, high);

2. Separately sort elements before
   partition and after partition
   QuickSort(arr, low, pi - 1);
```

```
QuickSort(arr, pi + 1, high);
```

6. **In-place sorting**:

Quick Sort is in-place as it does not use any extra storage while sorting. Merge Sort is out-of-place sort, it needs an extra space for temporary array.

Remember, the best choice of algorithm can vary based on specific project requirements, the characteristics of your data, and other factors.

2.7   Explain the Knapsack problem and how you would solve it.

The Knapsack problem is a combinatorial optimization problem that comes from a real-life situation in computer science.

Given a set of items, each with a weight and a value, determine the number of each item to include in a collection so that the total weight is less than or equal to a given limit and the total value is as large as possible. It derives its name from the problem faced by someone who is constrained by a fixed-size knapsack and must fill it with the most valuable items.

The problem is defined formally as follows:

- Inputs:

  - n items are given, each with a weight w[i] and a value v[i]
  - Maximum weight W

The task is to determine the maximum value that can be carried in the knapsack without exceeding weight W.

Here's a mathematical formulation of the problem:

$$\text{maximize: } \sum_{i=1}^{n} x_i \cdot v_i$$

$$\text{subject to: } \sum_{i=1}^{n} x_i \cdot w_i \leq W$$

$$\text{and: } x_i \in \{0, 1\} \quad \text{for all } i$$

The decision variable x_i is binary, indicating whether or not item i is included in the knapsack.

The problem can be solved by a dynamic programming algorithm:

1. Initialize a table K[][] of size n x W+1.

2. Build the table K[][] in bottom-up manner.

3. For each item i (from 1 to n):

- For each weight w (from 1 to W):

  - If w[i] <= w, then compute max(v[i] + K[i-1][w-w[i]], K[i-1][w])
  - Otherwise keep K[i-1][w]

The python code to solve the problem is as follows:

```
def knapSack(W, wt, val, n):
    K = [[0 for w in range(W+1)]
            for i in range(n+1)]
```

```
for i in range(n+1):
    for w in range(W+1):
        if i == 0 or w == 0:
            K[i][w] = 0
        elif wt[i-1] <= w:
            K[i][w] = max(val[i-1]
                + K[i-1][w-wt[i-1]],
                            K[i-1][w])
        else:
            K[i][w] = K[i-1][w]

return K[n][W]
```

You call this function as knapSack(W, wt, val, n) where:

- val[] is the array of values,

- wt[] is the array of weights,

- W is the knapsack's maximum weight,

- n is the number of items.

4. Return K[n][W] which contains the maximum value that can be carried in the knapsack.

This is a good solution but it is not efficient for large W (knapsack capacity). The time complexity of this algorithm is $O(nW)$ where n is the number of items and W is the knapsack capacity. Both time and space complexity of the dynamic programming solution is $O(nW)$. You should use this approach when the weight capacity is not too big.

2.8   How does the Floyd-Warshall algorithm work?

The Floyd-Warshall algorithm is a graph analysis algorithm for finding shortest paths in a weighted graph with positive or negative edge weights (but no negative cycles). It is a classic example of dynamic programming.

It works by incrementally improving an approximation to the shortest path distances. To see why it works, consider any shortest path from point i to j: such a path can either go directly from i to j (in the edge case that i = j, this is a path of length 0), or it can go through some intermediate points. The key insight is that if the path goes through some intermediate points, then the sub-path from i to the first intermediate point, and the sub-path from the last intermediate point to j, must themselves be shortest paths. In other words, we can build up shortest paths from shortest sub-paths.

Now let's express this in more formal terms:

- First, initialize your distance matrix with your adjacency matrix. Let's call this matrix $D[0]$. In $D[0][i][j]$, you store the distance from i to j (if there is an edge), or infinity (if there is no edge). The diagonal should be all 0, because the distance from any node to itself is 0.

- Then, iterate k from 1 to n, where n is the number of vertices. On each iteration, you construct a new matrix $D[k]$ from $D[k-1]$.

- To calculate the entries of $D[k]$, we use the following rule: $D[k][i][j]$ = min($D[k-1][i][j]$, $D[k-1][i][k]$ + $D[k-1][k][j]$). In other words, either the shortest path from i to j does not go through k, or it is cheaper to go from i to k and then from k to j.

Here's why this works: when we're filling in the $D[k]$ matrix, we're considering paths that only go through nodes 1 to k. At each step, we maintain the property that D[k][i][j] is the length of the shortest path from i to j that only goes through nodes 1 to k. By considering whether or not we go through k, we ensure that we consider all possible paths. A key insight is that all shortest paths with this property can be built by taking a shortest path with the same property that ends at k, and appending an edge from k to j.

The algorithm has the formula:

$$D_{ij}^{(k)} = min(D_{ij}^{(k-1)}, D_{ik}^{(k-1)} + D_{kj}^{(k-1)})$$

Here, $D_{ij}^{(k)}$ is the length of the shortest possible path from node i to node j over all paths that only use some subset of nodes $1, 2, ..., k$ as intermediate nodes.

By systematically applying this formula for $k = 1$ to n, and $i, j = 1$ to n at each step, we can compute the shortest paths between all pairs of nodes. The final result will be $D^{(n)}$. This will yield the shortest-path distances between all pairs of nodes, considering paths that use any subset of nodes as intermediate nodes.

The time complexity of this algorithm is $O(n^3)$, as it involves three nested loops over the number of vertices.

Here is a simple pseudo-code representation for the Floyd-Warshall algorithm:

```
Algorithm FloydWarshall(weights[][], n):
    initialize D as weights[][]
    for k from 1 to n
        let D_in_k_minus_1 = D
        for each i from 1 to n
            for each j from 1 to n
```

```
                    D[i][j] = min(D_in_k_minus_1[i][j] , D_in_k_minus_1[i
                       ][k] + D_in_k_minus_1[k][j])
     return D
```

At the end of this algorithm, D[i][j] holds the shortest distance
from node i to node j.

2.9 How would you find the shortest path in a graph?

Finding the shortest path in a graph is a popular problem in the
field of computer science. There are several algorithms to solve
this problem, and among them, Dijkstra's and Bellman-Ford's
algorithms are widely used.

Let's start with Dijkstra's algorithm, which is efficient and
works well with weighted graphs. However, it fails when dealing
with negative weights.

Here's a step-by-step outline of Dijkstra's algorithm:

1. Assign to each vertex a tentative distance value: set it to
zero for our initial vertex and to infinity for all other vertices.

2. Set the initial vertex as current. Mark all other vertices
unvisited. Create a set of all unvisited vertices.

3. For the current vertex, consider all its unvisited neighbors.
Calculate their tentative distances through the current vertex.
Compare the newly calculated tentative distance to the current
assigned value and assign the smaller one.

4. After considering all the neighboring vertices of the current

vertex, mark the current node as visited and remove it from the unvisited set. At this point, that node's shortest path will have been found.

5. Select the unvisited node with the smallest tentative distance, set it as the new "current node", and go back to step 3.

This continues until you've visited all the vertices in the graph, at which point you'll have the shortest path to each of them. The time complexity of Dijkstra's algorithm (when using a binary heap) is $\mathcal{O}((V+E)\log V)$ where V is the number of vertices and E is the number of edges.

However, as I mentioned earlier, Dijkstra's algorithm doesn't handle negative weights well. When negative weights are involved, you're likely better off using the Bellman-Ford algorithm.

Here's how the Bellman-Ford algorithm works:

1. Each vertex is assigned a distance: zero for the source vertex and infinity for all other vertices.

2. The algorithm goes through all the edges $V - 1$ times, where V is the number of vertices, updating the distances.

3. After the first $V - 1$ iterations, if the algorithm is able to update the distance, then it concludes that there is a negative-weight cycle.

The time complexity of the Bellman-Ford algorithm is $\mathcal{O}(V \cdot E)$.

The above approaches are often used in graph-related problems such as network routing, where you're trying to find the shortest distance from one node to all other nodes. That said, the approach can vary based on the specific requirements of the problem. Therefore, accurately identifying the problem and choosing the most suitable algorithm, taking into account their benefits and limitations, could be crucial for optimizing the solution.

2.10 How would you find all permutations of a string?

To find all permutations of a string, one common and efficient method is to use a recursive approach (backtracking). The idea is to fix a character at a time and swap the rest of the characters. This can be implemented as either returning a list of permutations, or printing them out directly. Here is the algorithm in pseudocode form:

- If the string has only one character, return the character itself.

- For each character in the string:

  - Fix the character.

  - Perform permutation for the remainder of the string.

  - Swap the fixed character with the rest of the characters of the string.

Pseudocode

```
function Permute(str, leftIndex, rightIndex)
    if leftIndex == rightIndex
        print str
    else
        for i from leftIndex to rightIndex
            str = Swap(str, leftIndex, i)
            Permute(str, leftIndex + 1, rightIndex)
```

```
str = Swap(str, leftIndex, i) // backtrack

function Swap(str, i , j)
   temp = str[i]
   str[i] = str[j]
   str[j] = temp
   return str
```

Here 'leftIndex' starts from index '0' and 'rightIndex' is 'str.length - 1'.

Python Implementation

To illustrate the above approach, let's take an example of Python function that generates all permutations for a given string:

```python
def get_permutations(s):
    if len(s) <= 1:
        return [s]

    perms = get_permutations(s[1:])
    first_char = s[0]
    result = []
    for perm in perms:
        for i in range(len(perm)+1):
            result.append(perm[:i] + first_char + perm[i:])
    return result
```

Given a string of 'n' characters, we can use the formula to calculate the total number of permutations as 'n¡ (n factorial), which means 'n*(n-1)*(n-2)*...*1'.

In computational complexity terms, the time and space complexity of generating all permutations of a string is 'O(n*n!)', making it quite inefficient on larger strings. This is due to the fact for every of the 'n¡ permutations, we do 'n' operations of string concatenation.

However, mathematics provides us with a beautiful solution to this complexity problem, namely Heap's Algorithm. Its implementation can efficiently generate all permutations of a finite sequence with a time complexity of 'O(n!)'. But it needs a deep understanding of permutations group in mathematics which is beyond the scope of this question.

Chapter 3

Time and Space Complexity Analysis

3.1 What is Big O notation and why is it important?

'Big O' notation, also known as asymptotic notation, is a mathematical notation that describes the limiting behavior of a function when the argument tends towards a particular value or infinity. In terms of computer science and coding, Big O notation is used for analyzing an algorithm's worst-case performance, denoting the maximum time taken, or the upper bound of time complexity.

The formal definition of Big O notation is:

Given two functions, 'f(n)' and 'g(n)', we say that 'f(n) = O(g(n))' if there exist constants 'c' > 0 and 'n0' 0 such that:

'$|f(n)|$ c * $|g(n)|$' for all 'n > n0'.

Let me put what this equation means in human words. "f(n) = O(g(n))" means "f(n) grows no faster than g(n)" in an asymptotics sense. Here, 'f(n)' is usually the time or space complexity function of an algorithm, and 'g(n)' is a simple function like '1', 'n', 'n^2', 'n * log(n)', etc.

Big O notation is important for the following reasons:

1. It helps us analyze the time and space efficiency of algorithms, this is inevitably critical when dealing with large amounts of data, a common scenario in modern computing. If your data increases exponentially, an inefficient algorithm can make a program non-functional.

2. It provides a measure to describe the worst-case scenario, enabling us to understand the maximum resources the algorithm could require.

As an example consider a simple linear search function:

```
def linear_search(array, target):
    for i in range(len(array)):
        if array[i] == target:
            return i
    return None
```

This function has a time complexity of O(n), as in the worst-case scenario, the target is at the last of the array, and the function has to iterate through every element.

In summary, Big O is critical in computer science because it provides a rough estimation of how an algorithm will perform as we scale the data it's operating on. This enables us to design and choose the most efficient algorithms for the specific applications we are developing.

3.2 Explain the difference between time complexity and space complexity.

Time complexity and space complexity are two ways of evaluating the efficiency of an algorithm. However, they measure two fundamentally different things.

Time Complexity

Time complexity is a measure of the total time required by an algorithm to complete its execution. In other words, it measures the amount of computer time that an algorithm needs to process input data of a given size.

We typically express time complexity using Big O notation. This notation provides a high-level analysis of the algorithm's efficiency by describing the worst-case scenario, i.e., the maximum time needed for execution as the size of the input data approaches infinity.

For example, consider an algorithm that checks whether a number is prime by dividing it by every number up to its square root. The time complexity would be $O(sqrt(n))$, where n is the number being checked, because the algorithm's time requirement increases in proportion to the square root of the size of the input data.

Space Complexity

Space complexity, on the other hand, measures the amount of

memory an algorithm needs to execute. It includes both the space required to hold the input data as well as any additional space the algorithm might require to hold intermediate results or output data.

Just like time complexity, space complexity is often expressed using Big O notation to represent the worst-case scenario.

For instance, consider an algorithm that generates all permutations of a given string. Since it needs to store all permutations at once, it requires an amount of space proportional to the factorial of the length of the string. Therefore, its space complexity would be $O(n!)$, where n is the length of the string.

Time-Space Trade-off

In many cases, there's a trade-off between time and space complexity. That is, you can often make an algorithm run faster by having it use more memory (a lookup table, for example), or make an algorithm use less memory by having it take more time.

Here is a small table chart to show the common complexities:

```
| Big O Notation     | Name        |
| -------------- |:--------------:|
| O(1)      | Constant |
| O(log n)    | Logarithmic |
| O(n) | Linear |
| O(n log n)     | Linear Logarithmic |
| O($n^2$)    | Quadratic |
| O($n^3$)     | Cubic |
| O($2^n$) | Exponential |
| O(n!) | Factorial |
```

It is worth mentioning that when analyzing an algorithm, understanding time and space complexity is important not just to quantify the total time or space an algorithm uses, but to .

understand how those quantities change as the size of the input data changes.

3.3 How do you determine the time complexity of a recursive function?

The time complexity of recursive functions is a little different than iterative functions. The time complexity of a recursive function is determined by the "Master Theorem".

The Master Theorem

Given a recursive relation every function of the following type:

```
T(n) = a*T(n/b) + f(n)
```

We can determine the time complexity by comparing f(n) with $n^l og_b(a)$:

- If f(n) is $O(n^c)$, where $c < log_b(a)$, then the time complexity is $\Theta(n^{log_b(a)})$.
- If f(n) is $\Theta(n^c * log^k(n))$ where $c = log_b(a)$, (for some k   0), then time complexity is $\Theta(n^c * log^(k+1)(n))$
- If f(n) is $\Omega(n^c)$, where $c > log_b(a)$, if $a * f(n/b) \leq k * f(n)$ for some constant k < 1 and sufficiently large n, then time complexity is $\Theta(f(n))$.

Let's look at examples for each.

Example 1:

```
T(n) = 2T(n/2) + n
```

Here, a=2, b=2, and f(n)=n. We have $c = log_b(a) = log_2(2) = 1$. In this case, $f(n) = n = n^c$, so we are in the second situation of the Master Theorem. Thus, the time complexity is:

$$(n^c * log^{(k+1)}(n)) = (n * log(n)) \tag{3.1}$$

Here, k=0 as there no log term with f(n).

Example 2:

```
T(n) = 2T(n/2) + log(n)
```

Again, a=2, b=2 but this time f(n)=log(n). Thus c, still 1<log(n) which means we are in the first situation of the Master Theorem. Hence, the time complexity would be $(n^{log_b(a)}) = (n)$.

Example 3:

```
T(n) = 2T(n/2) + n^2
```

Here, a=2, b=2, and $f(n) = n^2$. Hence $c = 2 > log_b(a) = 1$. Following the rules of Master theorem, we are now in the third case of the Master Theorem. For that, we must ensure that $a * f(n/b) \leq k * f(n)$. We find that $f(n/b) = n^2/4$ and $a * f(n/b) = 2 * (n^2/4)$ which is $1/2 * n^2$ that is less than n^2 for sufficiently large n. Thus, the Master theorem applies here and the time complexity is $(f(n)) = (n^2)$.

Please note that the Master Theorem covers many, but not all, recurrences. There can be situations where the given form does not meet any condition of the Master Theorem.

3.4   What is the time complexity of a hash table insert operation?

In the ideal case, the time complexity of a hash table insert operation is $O(1)$, or constant time. This is under the assumption that the hash function distributes the elements evenly across the hash table buckets, thereby avoiding or minimizing collisions, and that the size of the hash table is sufficient to accommodate the elements without having to perform resizing operations frequently.

Practically, collisions can occur where two different elements are hashed to the same index. To handle collisions, various techniques can be used like chaining or open addressing which may add an overhead.

Chaining: Each slot in the hash table holds a linked list of elements that hash to the same slot. The time complexity would be $O(n)$ in worst case scenario where all elements hash to the same slot, effectively creating a linked list.

Open Addressing: Elements are probed into next slots upon collision. In the worst case scenario (hash table almost full), it could potentially have to probe through much/most of the table, giving a time complexity of $O(n)$.

However, even considering collision handling, hash table operations are remarkably efficient if we can assume the hash function is well-designed, and given a large enough hash table, the time complexity of an insert operation still approximates to $O(1)$, on an average case.

Note, when the hash table reaches a certain load factor (ratio of number of items / table size), we may need to resize the hash table (usually doubling its size) and rehash all the items. This is an O(n) operation, but it is amortized over n insertions, so it doesn't affect the average time complexity of an individual insertion operation. Its effect becomes constant when spread over the individual insertions that triggered the resizing, hence we can still say the time complexity of a hash table insert operation is generally regarded as O(1).

The time complexity for the operations can be expressed as:

- Average Case: $O(1)$
- Worst Case: $O(n)$

Where "n" is the number of entries in the hash table.

3.5   What is the time and space complexity of Quick Sort?

Quick sort is an efficient in-place sorting algorithm. It's a divide and conquer algorithm that works by selecting a 'pivot' element from an array and partitioning the other elements into two sub-arrays according to whether they are less than or greater than the pivot. The sub-arrays are then recursively sorted.

Time Complexity:

In the best case (which occurs when the pivot element is always the median), the partitioning steps will result in subarrays of equal size (or nearly equal), achieving a balanced recursion tree. In this case, the time complexity is O(n log n), where n is the number of elements in the array.

The worst-case scenario occurs when the pivot is either the smallest or largest element in the array, which leads to a highly unbalanced partition and a worst-case time complexity of $O(n^2)$.

The average case time complexity of quicksort is also O(n log n), but it tends to be faster in practice than other O(n log n) algorithms, because its inner loop can be efficiently implemented on most architectures, and in most real-world data, it performs significantly better than other divide-and-conquer methods.

Space Complexity:

Quick sort is an in-place sorting algorithm but needs stack space for recursion. Specifically, a quicksort can operate in O(log n) space.

To sum up, these are the time complexities under different scenarios:

- Worst-case performance: $O(n^2)$

- Best-case performance: $O(n \log n)$

- Average performance: $O(n \log n)$

- Worst-case space complexity: $O(n)$ auxiliary (naive) or $O(\log n)$ auxiliary (Sedgewick 1978)

3.6 Explain how time and space complexity would influence your choice of algorithm.

When choosing an algorithm to solve a problem, the most important criteria generally revolve around its efficiency, in terms of both time complexity and space complexity.

Time complexity refers to the computational complexity that describes the amount of computational time taken by an algorithm to run, as a function of the size of the input to the program. It usually measures the number of steps required to complete the execution of an algorithm.

Space complexity is a measure of the amount of memory an algorithm needs to run to completion. It determines how much space a program or algorithm requires to perform its application perfectly.

The efficiency of an algorithm can be calculated by both these measures. An algorithm that solves a problem in less time and occupies lesser memory is considered good. If an algorithm requires a large amount of space but finishes quicker, or if it requires less space but takes a long time to complete, then it might not be considered efficient.

For example, let's consider the following two algorithms for finding an item in an unsorted list:

1. **Linear Search Algorithm**: This algorithm searches for an item in the list sequentially. If there are 'n' elements in the list, in the worst-case scenario, you might have to check all the 'n' elements. Therefore, its time complexity is 'O(n)'. However, since it doesn't require any extra space to run, the space complexity is 'O(1)'.

2. **Binary Search Algorithm**: This algorithm, however, requires the list to be sorted first, but it reduces the time complexity significantly. It repeatedly divides the list in half until it finds the item or the subarray size becomes 0. Therefore, its

time complexity is 'O(log n)'. Similar to the linear search, the Binary Search also doesn't require extra space and hence its space complexity is also 'O(1)'.

From a purely time complexity perspective, the Binary Search algorithm is better. However, Binary Search requires the input list to be sorted. Sorting an unsorted list can take 'O(n log n)' time in the best case (using the best sorting algorithms, such as Merge Sort, Heap Sort).

So, if the input list is sorted, Binary Search would be a better choice. If the list isn't sorted, and processing time is a critical factor, it might be a better move to use the Linear Search algorithm or sort the list first, then use the Binary Search depending on the frequency of the search operation.

In conclusion, neither time complexity nor space complexity alone could determine the most suitable algorithm. It depends on the constraints of your environment like memory available, expected input sizes, and requirement about time efficiency. Sometimes, there might be a scenario where we have to choose a tradeoff between time and space complexity. In a memory-constrained environment, it might make sense to choose an algorithm which is slower but uses less memory. On the other hand, in a speed-critical setup, an algorithm which runs faster but uses more memory might be the right choice.

3.7 How does the time complexity of an algorithm affect the performance?

The time complexity of an algorithm quantifies the amount of time an algorithm takes to run as a function of the size of the input to the program. It is usually estimated by counting the number of elementary operations performed by the algorithm, assuming that each elementary operation takes a fixed amount of time to perform. Therefore, the time complexity effectively measures how the run time grows — more or less — as the size of input increases.

To illustrate this, let's consider a simple function that sums up all numbers in a list. Here's the function in Python:

```python
def sum_numbers(lst):
    result = 0
    for x in lst:
        result += x
    return result
```

In the above function, the time complexity is O(n) (often referred to as linear time complexity) where 'n' is the length of the list 'lst'. This is because each additional element in the list will take a constant amount of time to process.

Conversely, if you have a function that must compare every element to every other element (say, to find duplicates), you are looking at a time complexity of $O(n^2)$ (often referred to as quadratic time complexity). Here's an example function:

```python
def has_duplicates(lst):
    n = len(lst)
    for i in range(n):
        for j in range(i+1, n):
            if lst[i] == lst[j]:
                return True
    return False
```

In the above function, each addition to the list 'lst' can potentially create a new comparison to be done with all the other elements in the list.

In terms of performance, an algorithm that has lower time complexity will generally be faster than an algorithm with higher time complexity, especially as the input size becomes larger.

Here's a simple chart showing the growth rates for different time complexities:

```
Time complexity Growth rate
O(1)            Constant
O(log n)        Logarithmic
O(n)            Linear
O(n log n)      Log linear
O(n^2)          Quadratic
O(n^3)          Cubic
O(2^n)          Exponential
```

You can see that as we move down the table, the growth rate increases substantially. With large inputs, a time complexity difference can mean the difference between a result in a sensible time or waiting too long to ever see the result.

Please note that time complexity doesn't tell the whole story; there are other factors at play, such as the space complexity (the amount of memory an algorithm uses), the programming language and environment, the constant factors in the time complexity (which are ignored in Big O notation but can matter in practice), and so on. But it's a good starting point for analyzing the performance of an algorithm.

3.8 What does O(log n) mean, and can you give an example of an algorithm with this time complexity?

'O(log n)' refers to a logarithmic time complexity in the big O notation. This implies that the running time of an algorithm increases logarithmically in proportion to the size of the input data set.

Logarithmic time refers to an algorithm that improves performance as the data set increases. These algorithms apply to scenarios where an algorithm repeatedly reduces the size of the input data to achieve a result, such as in a binary search.

The most standard example of an algorithm with an 'O(log n)' time complexity is indeed the binary search algorithm.

Binary Search Algorithm

The binary search algorithm is a search algorithm that finds the location of a target value within a sorted array. It compares the target value to the middle element of the array and, based on that comparison, can disregard half of the array. Given sorted elements, the algorithm continues to divide the search space in half until the target value is found.

Here's a simple implementation of Binary Search in Python:

```python
def binary_search(arr, low, high, x):
    if high >= low:
        mid = (high + low) // 2

        if arr[mid] == x:
            return mid

        elif arr[mid] > x:
            return binary_search(arr, low, mid - 1, x)

        else:
            return binary_search(arr, mid + 1, high, x)

    else:
        return -1
```

Proof of Time Complexity of Binary Search:

Our task is to find one element in an array of size 'n'. Let's denote 'T(n)' as the number of comparisons in the worst case for an array of size 'n'.

As we are dividing array in half at each step, the relation we get is:

$$T(n) = T(n/2) + 1$$

This is a recurrence relation. Solving it yields 'T(n) = O(log n)'.

The '+1' in the recurrence relationship stems from the fact that each operation (i.e., checking the midpoint of the array/sub-array) takes constant 'O(1)' time.

In other words, if we have 'n' elements, in the worst case we need:

- 1 iteration to halve 'n' elements to 'n/2'
- 1 iteration to halve 'n/2' elements to 'n/4'
- and so on...

Continuing this process, we see that the maximum number of iterations to find a value, or realize it is not in the array, is the number of times you can halve the 'n', plus one, which mathematically equals '$\log_2 n + 1$'.

This proves that Binary Search is an 'O(log n)' operation in the worst case scenario.

It's important to stress again that, because the run-time complexity of Binary Search is 'log n', it's one of the most efficient algorithms we have in computer science. The difference becomes especially apparent for large numbers.

3.9   How would you reduce the space complexity of a given algorithm?

Space complexity refers to the total amount of computer memory taken up during the execution of an algorithm. Optimizing it can make your code faster and more efficient. Here are several strategies to decrease the space complexity:

1. **Limit Variable Usage**: Classify which variables truly need all-function scope or might be reassigned lesser, local scopes. E.g., rather than utilizing global variables, use local variables whenever possible.

Compare:

```
int global_var;

void function(...) {
    ...
    global_var = some_value;
    ...
}
```

To:

```
void function(...) {
    ...
    int local_var = some_value;
    ...
}
```

2. **Use Iterative Methods Over Recursive**: Recursive methods often require more space because of the need to remember multiple function calls. Iterative solutions, on the other hand, usually need less space because they execute a set of instruc-

tions in a loop without requiring additional memory for each iteration. E.g.:

Recursive:

```
int factorial(int n) {
    if (n == 0)
        return 1;
    else
        return n * factorial(n - 1);
}
```

Iterative:

```
int factorial(int n) {
  int result = 1;
  for (int i = 1; i <= n; i++) {
    result *= i;
  }
  return result;
}
```

3. **Reuse Memory for Variables**: Instead of creating new variables for each time you need them, try to reuse the old variables that have already served their purpose.

4. **Efficient Data Structures**: Use data structures like an array, linked list, stack, queue, hash table, etc., wisely. For example, if we only need to store unique elements then hash-table or set can be much more efficient compare to a simple list or array.

Compare this:

```
List<String> list = new ArrayList<String>();
...
list.add("new element");
```

To this:

```
Set<String> set = new HashSet<String>();
...
```

```
set.add("new␣element");
```

5. **In-Place Algorithms**: These algorithms modify the input
data structure such that they consume minimal extra space, and
the output is typically created in the input data structure itself.

Optimizing space complexity not only conserves memory resources but also may result in faster programs, due to reduced
memory allocation and deallocation, as well as reduced garbage
collection.

3.10 What is the worst-case and average-case complexity of a binary search tree?

Binary Search Trees (BTS) have various levels of time complexity for their operations such as search, insert, and delete.

1. **Worst Case**: In the worst-case scenario, a binary search
tree can become skewed in either direction (left or right- skewed).
That means, each parent node has only one child node. This
forms a linear structure similar to a linked list. In such a case,
the operations on BST could take 'O(n) time'. Here 'n' is the
number of nodes, because we may have to traverse through all
the nodes.

For example, if we have a tree like this:

```
50
  \
   70
     \
```

```
80
  \
   90
```

Search, insertion or deletion will require to go through all the nodes, hence time complexity is 'O(n)'.

2. **Average Case**: The average-case time complexity in a balanced binary search tree is 'O(log n)'. In a balanced BST, the tree is very much 'balanced', each left and right subtree contains an approximately equal number of nodes. As a result, the height of the tree remains small (logarithmic in relation to the number of nodes).

The operations of search, insert, delete operations can be performed in 'O(log n)' time. This happens because you are essentially discarding half of the tree at each level (since you're able to decide whether the target value would reside in the left or the right subtree).

For example, consider a balanced BST with 7 nodes:

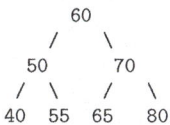

```
     60
   /    \
  50      70
 / \     / \
40  55  65  80
```

If you want to search for the number 55, you can tell at each step which child node may contain this number, allowing discarding half part in each step, hence the time complexity is 'O(log n)'.

Please note that to maintain the average time complexity for a Binary search tree, it is crucial to keep the tree balanced, such as in an AVL tree or Red-Black tree.

To put it in terms of big thema, in the worst case, the complexity of a binary search tree operation is 'O(n)'. However, in an average case, this becomes 'O(log n)'.

Chapter 4

Array and String Problems

4.1 How would you reverse a string?

Reversing a string is a fundamental problem in computer programming and interviewers often ask this question to test one's understanding of basic string manipulation. There are different ways to reverse a string in various languages, but for this question, I'll demonstrate using Python because of its simplicity and readability.

Here is a straightforward solution using Python's slicing syntax:

```
def reverse_string(input_str):
    return input_str[::-1]
```

In the above code, '[::-1]' is a slice that steps backwards, -1 step

at a time, through the entire string. This effectively reverses
the string.

But if you must write it from scratch without using language
built-in functions, you could follow these steps:

- Define a function that takes a string as input.

- Initialize an empty string as a variable where you will store the
reversed string.

- Loop through the input string from the end to the beginning.

- In each iteration append current character to the reversed string.

Here's what the code would look like in Python:

```python
def reverse_string(str):
    reversed_str = ''
    for i in range(len(str) - 1, -1, -1):
        reversed_str += str[i]
    return reversed_str
```

Another way to reverse a string, which is often seen in an interview setup, is using a stack. This method is due to the LIFO
(Last In First Out) property of the stack data structure.

Here's what the code would look like in Python:

```python
def reverse_stringStack(input_str):
    stack = list(input_str)
    result = ''
    while len(stack):
        result += stack.pop()
    return result
```

In the above code:

- We convert the input string to a list (i.e., a stack in Python).

- We then pop the elements from the stack one by one (which will
pop from the end of the list) and append it into the result string.

- We keep doing this until the stack is empty, and return the result string which will be the reversed input string.

Please note that the time complexity for these solutions is O(n), where n is the length of the string.

4.2   Can you find all the permutations of a given string?

Finding all the permutations of a given string is a common problem in computer programming and can be solved using recursion and backtracking.

Here is a Python code snippet that accomplishes this:

```python
def permute(data, i, length):
    if i==length:
        print(''.join(data))
    else:
        for j in range(i, length):
            data[i], data[j] = data[j], data[i]
            permute(data, i+1, length)
            data[i], data[j] = data[j], data[i]

string = 'ABC'
n = len(string)
data = list(string)
permute(data, 0, n)
```

The function 'permute' generates all the permutations of a string. This is done by swapping each character in the string with every other character (including itself). For each swap, 'permute' is called recursively with the next character, until all characters have been used. The swapped characters are then swapped back to their original positions before the next iteration.

This process can be better understood with the following tree diagram:

```
ABC
/ | \
A BC ACB
/ \ / \
AB C AC B
/ \ / \
ABC ACB ABC ACB
```

In the diagram above, each level of the tree corresponds to a character position in the string. Each node represents a string permutation. When the tree is fully expanded, all possible permutations are printed.

There are n! permutations in a string of length n. This is because there are n choices for the first character, n-1 choices for the second character, n-2 choices for the third character, and so on, until only 1 choice is left for the last character. This can be represented mathematically as:

$$n! = n * (n-1) * (n-2) * \ldots * 2 * 1.$$

Also, for each permutation, there are n*(n-1) swaps made, so the time complexity of this algorithm is $O(n^2 * n!)$.

4.3 How would you check if a string is a palindrome?

A palindrome is a word, phrase, number, or other sequences of characters that reads the same backward as forward, ignoring spaces, punctuation, and capitalization.

One way of checking whether a string is palindrome or not is by comparing the characters at each end of the string and work your way towards the middle of the string. If the characters match for each comparison, then the string is a palindrome. Here is a simple Python function for checking if a string is a palindrome.

```python
def is_palindrome(s):
    # Convert string to lowercase, remove non-alphanumeric
        characters
    s = ''.join(c for c in s.lower() if c.isalnum())
    return s == s[::-1]

print(is_palindrome("A man, a plan, a canal: Panama")) # returns
    True
print(is_palindrome("race a car")) # returns False
```

If you want a more manual implementation without the use of python's built-in methods, you could also do:

```python
def is_palindrome(s):
    j = len(s)-1
    for i in range (len(s) // 2):
        if(s[i] != s[j-i]):
            return False
    return True
```

where 'i' is the starting index and 'j' is the last index of the array. The condition part of the loop will make the function to return 'false' as soon as the comparison fails and 'true' if both the parts are successfully same after full comparison of 'i' from start and 'j' from the end.

For example:

When you input: 'is_palindrome("MADAM")', in the first iteration, 's[0] ('M')' compares with 's[4] ('M')' which are equal and then 's[1] ('A')' with 's[3] ('A')', so after full comparison it returns 'true' as they are a palindrome.

When you input: 'is_palindrome("Hello")', in the first iteration, 's[0]('H')' compares with 's[4]('o')' which are not equal
so at the first comparison it returns 'false' as they are not a
palindrome.

The purpose of 'len(s)//2' is to avoid over-checking in palin-
dromes with an odd number of characters. This makes the
solution efficient with the time complexity of O(N), where N is
the length of the string. No additional space is used, making
the space complexity O(1).

The Python '[::-1]' does a complete slice over the string in reverse, i.e., the string is completely reversed which allows us to
do a equality check on the original and reverse string. This
is another clever technique to identify a palindrome in Python
though it doesn't really show the manual process of comparing
character by character from either end towards the center. The
time complexity also remains O(N).

4.4   How do you find the first non-repeating character in a string?

Finding the first non-repeating character in a string is a problem
that can be solved using hashing. The basic idea is to get the
frequency count of all the characters and find the one with a
count of 1.

Here are the steps in Python:

1. Create a hash table to store the count of each character in

the string as 'charCount'. The key will be the character itself and the value is the count.

2. Iterate through the string in order (this is important as we are looking for the first non-repeating character). As we go, add the characters to the 'charCount' hash table and increment their count value.

3. After we have counted all characters, iterate through the string in the original order again. This time, check the 'charCount' for each character. Return the first character that has a count of 1.

Here's an example code:

```
def firstUniqChar(s):
    charCount = {}

    # Get character count.
    for c in s:
        if c not in charCount:
            charCount[c] = 1
        else:
            charCount[c] += 1

    # Find the first non-repeating character.
    for c in s:
        if charCount[c] == 1:
            return c

    return None
```

You can test it with some string:

```
print(firstUniqChar('interviewQuery')) # returns 'i'
print(firstUniqChar('codesignal')) # returns 'c'
```

Note that this solution assumes that the string contains only ASCII characters. If the string can contain any unicode characters then the hash table needs to be updated to accommodate these.

This solution has a time complexity of $O(n)$ where n is the size of the string. This is because we perform a single pass to count the characters, and a second pass to find the first unique character. The space complexity is also $O(n)$ for the storage required for the hash table.

4.5   Can you remove duplicates from a sorted array?

Duplicates from a sorted array can be removed. One common and efficient method used to do this is the Two Pointers method.

Two Pointers Method

The key idea behind this method is to have one pointer 'fast' scan through the array, and another pointer 'slow' move only if we find a number not seen before. By the end of the process, the part in the array before 'slow' will be all the unique elements in the sorted array.

Let's go through an example to clarify this:

Suppose we have an input array 'nums' sorted in non-decreasing order such as 'nums = [0,0,1,1,1,2,2,3,3,4]'

We start with 'fast' and 'slow' pointers, both initialized at the first index of the array.

Here is a step by step guide of how to do it:

1. Compare the element pointed to by 'fast' with the element before 'slow' (since it's the last confirmed unique element).

2. If they're different, increment 'slow' and then copy the element at 'fast' into 'slow'.

3. Increment 'fast'.

4. Repeat the above steps until 'fast' reaches the end of the array.

In the end, 'slow + 1' will be the new length of the array without duplicates.

Below is the corresponding Python code:

```
def removeDuplicates(nums):
    if not nums:
        return 0

    slow = 0
    for fast in range(1, len(nums)):
        if nums[fast] != nums[slow]:
            slow += 1
            nums[slow] = nums[fast]

    return slow + 1
```

In the sample input array 'nums = [0,0,1,1,1,2,2,3,3,4]', if we run the 'removeDuplicates' function, it will return '5', and the first five elements of 'nums' will be '[0, 1, 2, 3, 4]', which are the unique elements.

This algorithm has a time complexity of 'O(n)', where 'n' is the length of the array, and space complexity of 'O(1)' as it operates in-place.

4.6 How would you find the missing number in a sequence?

There are several types of sequences you might encounter, including arithmetic sequences, geometric sequences, and more

complex series. The method for finding the missing number
will depend on the type of series. Let's walk through methods
for both arithmetic and geometric sequences as examples.

1. **Arithmetic sequences**: In an arithmetic sequence, the
difference between consecutive terms is the same. If you're given
such sequence and there is a missing term, you can use the
formula for the nth term of an arithmetic sequence to find it:

$$a_n = a_1 + (n - 1) * d$$

where a_n is the nth term, a_1 is the first term, n is the position
of the term in the sequence, and d is the common difference.

For example, if you have a sequence 4, _, 8, you know that
$d = 2$ because the difference between 8 and 4 is 4. The missing
term is the second term, so $n = 2$. Plugging in these values:

$$a_2 = 4 + (2 - 1) * 2 = 6$$

So 6 is the missing number.

2. **Geometric sequences**: In a geometric sequence, the ratio
between consecutive terms is the same. If there is a missing
number, you can use the formula for the nth term of a geometric
sequence to find it:

$$a_n = a_1 * r^{(n-1)}$$

where a_n is the nth term, a_1 is the first term, n is the position
of the term in the sequence, and r is the common ratio.

For example, in a sequence 2, _, 8, you can see that the common ratio is 4. The missing number is the second term, so $n = 2$. Plugging in these values:

$$a_2 = 2 * 4^{(2-1)} = 8$$

However, this result contradicts our sequence, so we may have assumed the wrong ratio. Since geometric sequences multiply by a common ratio, it's quite possible that our ratio is, in fact, the square root of 4, which is 2. Let's try that:

$$a_2 = 2 * 2^{(2-1)} = 4$$

And so, 4 is the missing number in the geometric sequence.

Remember, these are just two examples — if you have a more complex series or other types of number sequences, there may be different rules to identify and deal with them.

4.7 Can you rotate a matrix 90 degrees?

You can rotate a matrix 90 degrees clockwise. In programming, this is a common question in coding interviews because it tests your ability to work with multi-dimensional arrays.

To achieve this, you just need to understand the pattern. When a matrix is rotated 90 degrees, the first row becomes the last column, the second row becomes the second last column, and so on.

There are several methods to achieve this task and here is a simple and intuitive method using extra space.

Let's say we have a matrix 'm' and its dimensions are 'n'x'n'. We start from the top row, we take the elements of the top row and place them in the last column in the same order. We take the elements from the second row and place them in the second last column in the same order and so on.

Here's the pseudocode for the process:

```
Let A be the original matrix
Let n be the dimension of the matrix
Let B be a new n x n matrix

For i from 0 to n-1
 For j from 0 to n-1
  B[j][n-1-i] = A[i][j]
```

Here's how it works on a 3x3 matrix for example:

Suppose A is:

```
A = 1 2 3
    4 5 6
    7 8 9
```

The rotated matrix B is:

```
B = 7 4 1
    8 5 2
    9 6 3
```

For any element A[i][j] in the original matrix, it will go to position B[j][n - 1 - i] in the rotated matrix.

If you need to rotate the matrix in-place (without allocating extra space), the solution is a bit more complex as you need to do the rotation in a cycle-wise manner. That is often the follow-up question in coding interviews.

4.8 How would you find the maximum subarray sum?

Finding the maximum subarray sum is a common algorithmic problem that can be solved using algorithms such as Kadane's algorithm. Before we get into that, let's understand what is a subarray. A subarray is a contiguous part of an array. Hence, in the problem, we are looking for a contiguous subarray within a one-dimensional array of numbers which has the largest sum.

Let's discuss how Kadane's algorithm works:

1. Initialize:

  - max_so_far = 0

  - max_ending_here = 0

2. Loop over each element of the array (Let the current element in loop be 'x')

  - max_ending_here = max_ending_here + x

  - if max_ending_here < 0 max_ending_here = 0

  - if max_so_far < max_ending_here max_so_far = max_ending_here

3. return max_so_far

In the algorithm, max_so_far stores the maximum subarray sum encountered so far. And, max_ending_here stores the sum of the current subarray. If at some point in time, we get max_ending_here < 0, we start looking for a new subarray - as the current subarray ends.

In terms of time complexity, this algorithm runs in O(N) where

N is the number of elements in the input array. This is because
Kadane's algorithm needs just one loop through the array, so
it is quite time efficient.

Here is an example code snippet in Python:

```
def max_subarray_sum(arr):
  size = len(arr)

  max_so_far = max_ending_here = 0

  for i in range(0, size):
    max_ending_here = max_ending_here + arr[i]

    if max_ending_here < 0:
      max_ending_here = 0

    if max_so_far < max_ending_here:
      max_so_far = max_ending_here

  return max_so_far
```

Now, to demonstrate its working let's consider 'arr = [-2, 1, -3,
4, -1, 2, 1, -5, 4]'

Loop through the array and on each iteration;

- add the current element to max_ending_here, '-2' at i=0.

- Then compare this sum with 0. If it is less than 0, reset
max_ending_here to 0. So in the first iteration with '-2',
max_ending_here becomes 0

- Then compare max_so_far with max_ending_here, if
max_ending_here is greater, replace max_so_far with it.

- Run this loop for the length of the array and at the end,
max_so_far will hold the maximum sum.

After going through all the elements in the array, we'll end up
with max_so_far = '6', which indeed is the maximum sum

subarray '[4, -1, 2, 1]'.

4.9   Can you find the longest common prefix in an array of strings?

You can find the longest common prefix in an array of strings by using a character by character matching method. The algorithm starts with the first character and continues to the next character only if all the strings have the same character at the current position.

The time complexity of this approach is approximately O(N*M), where N is the number of strings, and M is the length of the largest string string in the array.

Algorithm:

1. Initialize a string 'prefix' as the first string in the array.

2. Iterate through the array, and for each string, check whether it has 'prefix' as a prefix. If not, shorten 'prefix' by excluding the last character and proceed to the next string.

3. Repeat step 2 until either 'prefix' becomes empty or it is a prefix of all the strings in the array.

4. Return 'prefix'.

Here is a Python example of the above algorithm:

```
def longestCommonPrefix(strs):
    if not strs:
        return ""

    prefix = strs[0]
    for string in strs[1:]:
        while not string.startswith(prefix):
            prefix = prefix[:-1]
```

```
        if not prefix:
            return ""
    return prefix
```

For an array of strings 'strs = ["flower","flow","flight"]', the longest common prefix is "fl".

Please note that as this algorithm checks character by character from the beginning of each string, as soon as the strings no longer have a common character the algorithm stops, making it very efficient even for large lists of strings.

4.10 How would you move all zeros in an array to the end?

Moving all zeros in an array to the end can be achieved through an algorithmic technique called "two-pointer technique". Following the steps below will accomplish this:

1. Initialize two pointers 'i' and 'j' to 0.

2. Run a while-loop until 'i' reaches the end of the array.

3. If the array[i] is non-zero, swap the array[i] and array[j] and increment both 'i' and 'j'.

4. If the array[i] is 0, increment 'i' only.

Here's corresponding Python code and explanation:

```
def move_zeros_to_end(arr):
    n = len(arr)

    j = 0 # Count of non-zero elements
    for i in range(n):
        # If element at index i is non-zero, then replace the element
        # at index j with this element
```

```
if arr[i] != 0:
    # Swap
    arr[j], arr[i] = arr[i], arr[j]
    # increment count of non-zero elements
    j += 1

return arr
```

You could call the function with your array, like so:

```
arr = [1, 0, 2, 0, 3, 0, 0, 4, 5]
print(move_zeros_to_end(arr))
```

This would result in:

```
Output: [1, 2, 3, 4, 5, 0, 0, 0, 0]
```

The time complexity of the above algorithm is O(n) because the array is traversed once only. The space complexity is O(1), no extra space is used. Plus, this is an in-place algorithm which means original order of non-zero elements is maintained.

Here's a step-by-step illustration of how the algorithm works for the following input: $[1, 0, 2, 0, 3, 0, 0, 4, 5]$ i and j both start at index 0.

```
arr: [1, 0, 2, 0, 3, 0, 0, 4, 5]
      i
      j
```

Since 'arr[i]' is not zero, 'arr[j]' and 'arr[i]' are swapped and both 'i' and 'j' are incremented. Now our array and pointers both look like this:

```
arr: [1, 0, 2, 0, 3, 0, 0, 4, 5]
         i
         j
```

Since 'arr[i]' is zero, only the 'i' pointer will be incremented and thus the following state:

```
arr: [1, 0, 2, 0, 3, 0, 0, 4, 5]
               i
         j
```

The process continues similarly, with 'i' and 'j' pointers incrementing under different conditions until 'i' reaches the end of the array, with final result of '[1, 2, 3, 4, 5, 0, 0, 0, 0]'.

Chapter 5

Linked List Problems

5.1 How would you reverse a linked list?

Reversing a linked list involves changing the direction of next pointers in a linked list. This means if you have a linked list A -> B -> C -> D -> NULL, it should be turned into NULL <- A <- B <- C <- D.

Here is a simple algorithm demonstrating this often-solved problem:

Assume we have a class defining nodes:

```
class Node:
    def __init__(self, x):
        self.value = x
        self.next = None
```

We can solve the problem using iteration:

```
def reverseList(self, head):
    previous, current = None, head
    while current:
        next_node, current.next = current.next, previous
        previous, current = current, next_node
    return previous
```

Here, we:

1. Maintain two pointers: 'previous' initialized as 'None' and 'current' initialized as 'head'.

2. In every iteration, we update the 'next' pointer of the 'current' node to point to the 'previous' node.

3. Finally, we return the new 'head' of the linked list, which is the 'previous' pointer.

Now, let's break it down how the above iterative solution works:

Imagine initially

```
A->B->C->D->None
```

Let's take 'previous = None' and 'current = head' (A).

In the loop, we keep a reference to 'current.next' (B), then change 'current.next' to 'previous' (None), finally move 'previous' and 'current' one step forward.

Now it becomes

```
None<-A B->C->D->None
      previous current
```

Do the same steps again:

```
None<-A<-B C->D->None
         previous current
```

And it ends like this:

```
None<-A<-B<-C<-D
          previous(current)
```

When 'current' becomes 'None', it means we reached the tail of the original linked list (the new head of the reversed one). The algorithm returns 'previous', which points to the head of the reversed list.

We don't have to worry about losing the links between nodes. For example, when switching B and C, because before we change 'current.next', we've already saved the reference to it in 'next_node'.

As for the time complexity, this algorithm performs with O(n), where n represents the length of the linked list. This is because every node in the list is traversed exactly once.

Finally, please note that, although in-place reversal like this is common and neat, it's destructive – it destroys the original list by changing the node in place. If you need to keep the original list unchanged, you will need to clone the nodes.

5.2 Can you find the middle of a linked list?

We can certainly find the middle of a linked list using two pointer technique also known as the "Runner Technique".

This method involves initializing two pointers at the head of the list: a 'slow' pointer and a 'fast' pointer. The slow pointer will iterate one node at a time, while the fast pointer will move two nodes at once. When the 'fast' pointer reaches the end of the linked list, the 'slow' pointer will be at the middle.

Here's a Python example:

```python
class Node:
    def __init__(self, data=None):
        self.data = data
        self.next = None

def find_middle(head):
    slow = head
    fast = head
    while fast and fast.next:
        slow = slow.next
        fast = fast.next.next
    return slow.data

# Creating the linked list
head = Node(1)
head.next = Node(2)
head.next.next = Node(3)
head.next.next.next = Node(4)
head.next.next.next.next = Node(5)

# Find the middle
print(find_middle(head)) # Output: 3
```

This algorithm works in $O(n)$ time, where n is the length of the linked list, and in $O(1)$ space, because we're using a constant amount of space.

```python
class Node:
    def __init__(self, data=None):
        self.data = data
        self.next = None

def find_middle(head):
    slow = head
    fast = head
    while fast and fast.next:
        slow = slow.next
        fast = fast.next.next
    return slow.data
```

5.3   How would you detect a cycle in a linked list?

Detecting a cycle in a linked list is a common interview problem in computer science and it tests your knowledge on the data structure, especially linked lists, and algorithms.

Here are a couple of ways you can do this:

1. Hashing Method

The simplest way to detect a cycle in a linked list is by using a hash table. This method involves traversing the linked list one node at a time. For every node, check if it is in the hash table. If it is, then there is a cycle present. If the node is not in the hash table, add it and move to the next node.

Let us write the pseudo-code:

```
Initialize an empty hash table

For each node in the linked list:
   if the node is not in the hash table:
       add the node to the hash table
   else:
       return True // cycle detected

return False // cycle not detected
```

However, this method may not be efficient in terms of space complexity (in worst case, $O(n)$ where n is the number of nodes).

2. Floyd's Cycle Finding Algorithm (Two Pointers Method)

The second, more optimized solution involves using two pointers that traverse the list at different speeds (typically called 'slow' and 'fast' pointers). The 'slow' pointer moves one node at a time while the 'fast' pointer moves two nodes. If there is a cycle in the list, the 'fast' pointer will end up looping around and meeting the 'slow' pointer again. If there is no cycle, the 'fast' pointer will reach the end of the list.

Let us write the pseudo-code:

```
Initialize slow pointer to head of the list
Initialize fast pointer to head of the list

While fast pointer is not null and fast.next is not null:
  Move slow pointer one step
  Move fast pointer two steps

  if slow pointer is equal to fast pointer:
    return True   // cycle detected

return False   // cycle not detected
```

In this method, no additional space is required, hence the space complexity is constant O(1). This algorithm is also known as the "hare and tortoise" algorithm, because of the different speeds at which the pointers traverse the list.

Mathematical Representation

For Floyd's cycle finding algorithm, if we assume there is a cycle, and denote the distance from the head to the cycle start as 'x', the cycle length as 'y', and the distance from the cycle start to the meeting point of 'slow' and 'fast' as 'z'.

When 'slow' and 'fast' meet, we have:

distance traveled by slow $= x + z$

distance traveled by fast $= x + z + n \cdot y$ (n is the number of laps 'fast' has taken in the cycle)

Since 'fast' travels at twice the speed of 'slow', we get:

$2 \cdot (x + z) = x + z + n \cdot y$

Solving this, we get

$$x = (n - 1) \cdot y + (y - z)$$

which means:

- the distance from the head of the list to the start of the cycle is equal to

- the number of complete cycle rounds the fast pointer has made minus 1 times the cycle length plus

- the cycle length minus the distance of the meeting point from the start of the cycle.

If we start two pointers again from the meeting point and the head, they will meet at the start of the cycle since the distances they have to travel are exactly the same. This can be used to find the starting point of the cycle.

Both these algorithms are useful ways to detect cycles in linked lists, and the approach you choose can depend on the specific requirements of your problem, such as whether you have space limitations.

Please note that these solutions work mainly for singly-linked lists. For doubly-linked lists, we could take advantage of the backward link to solve the problem using different approaches.

5.4 Can you merge two sorted linked lists?

Two sorted linked lists can be merged. This problem is common in IT interviews, because it demonstrates the practical application of linked list data structures. The algorithm to merge

two sorted linked lists would generally be based on the "merge"
process used in merge sort.

One possible way to accomplish this is by using a iterative solution, as follows:

1. Create a new head node, 'mergedList'.

2. Keep track of the current node in the 'mergedList'.

3. Set two pointers ('list1Pointer' and 'list2Pointer') to the heads of
the two lists.

4. Compare the values at 'list1Pointer' and 'list2Pointer'.

5. Append the lesser value to 'mergedList'.

6. Repeat steps 4-5 until one of the pointers reaches the end of its
respective list.

7. Append the remainder of the non-empty list to 'mergedList'.

Here's the pseudocode for merging two linked lists:

```
function mergeLists(list1Pointer, list2Pointer):
    create a new node, mergedList
    set current to mergedList
    while list1Pointer is not null and list2Pointer is not null do
        if list1Pointer.value <= list2Pointer.value then
            current.next = new Node(list1Pointer.value)
            list1Pointer = list1Pointer.next
        else
            current.next = new Node(list2Pointer.value)
            list2Pointer = list2Pointer.next
        end if
        current = current.next
    end while
    if list1Pointer is not null then
        current.next = list1Pointer
    end if
    if list2Pointer is not null then
        current.next = list2Pointer
    end if
    return mergedList.next
end function
```

This pseudocode assumes a singly linked list where 'next' points
to the next node in the list, and 'null' signifies the end of the

list.

The time complexity of this algorithm is linear, i.e., $O(n + m)$, where 'n' and 'm' are the sizes of the two linked lists. This is because in the worst case, we need to traverse both linked lists fully to merge them. The space complexity is $O(1)$, as we are only using a constant amount of space to store the pointers.

Of course, this is just one method of merging two sorted linked lists. There are other ways of doing this, depending on the specific requirements of the problem, such as doing it in a recursive manner instead of using an iterative approach.

5.5 How would you remove a given node from a linked list?

To remove a specific node from a linked list, we first need to locate that node and then update the pointers accordingly. Here's a high-level algorithm for deleting a node from a linked list:

- If the head node is the one to be deleted,

  - Change the head pointer to the next of the current head.

- Else,

  - Initialize a 'previousNode' to point to the head node.

  - Traverse the linked list until the target node is found or the end of the list is reached.

  - Update the 'next' value of the 'previousNode' to point to the 'next' value of the target node.

Suppose we have a singly linked list and we want to remove a node 'n':

```
class Node {
    public int data;
    public Node next;
}

public void deleteNode(Node node, Node n) {
    if(node == n) {
        if(node.next == null) {
            System.out.println("There is only one node. The list can't
                be made empty ");
            return;
        }

        node.data = node.next.data;
        node.next = node.next.next;

        System.gc();

        return;
    }

    Node prev = node;
    while(prev.next != null && prev.next != n) {
        prev = prev.next;
    }

    if(prev.next == null) {
        System.out.println("Given node is not present in Linked List"
            );
        return;
    }

    prev.next = prev.next.next;

    System.gc();
    return;
}
```

Visualizing the process can better help show how node removal occurs in linked lists:

1- Linked List before removal:

```
---> [HEAD| ]---> [ | ]---> [TARGET| ]---> [ | ]---> NULL
```

2- Linked List after removing target:

```
---> [HEAD| ]---> [ | ] ----------------> [ | ]---> NULL
```

For doubly linked lists, the algorithm is slightly more complex because we have to update the 'previous' pointer of the node after the target node, but the overall concept is the same.

The time complexity for this operation is O(n) as at worst case, we need to traverse all elements in the linked list.

5.6   Can you find the kth to last element of a singly linked list?

Finding the kth to last element of a singly linked list is a common question in coding interviews. The key here is to observe that we do not have a direct access to the end of the linked list unless we traverse it once. With this observation, we can use the technique of maintaining two pointers that each starts at the head of the list. We move one pointer k steps forwards first, then we move both pointers at the same speed until the first pointer reaches the end. At that point, the second pointer will point to the kth to last element.

Here is a Python implementation of the algorithm:

```python
class ListNode:
    def __init__(self, x):
        self.val = x
        self.next = None


def find_kth_to_last(head, k):
    p1 = head
    p2 = head

    # Move p1 k nodes into the list
    for i in range(k):
        if p1 is None: return None # If k > length of the list
        p1 = p1.next
```

```
# Move p1 to the end, maintaining the gap
while p1:
    p1 = p1.next
    p2 = p2.next

# Now, p2 points to kth to last element
return p2.val
```

In this sample code, the linked list is represented by a 'ListNode' where 'val' is the value of the node and 'next' is a pointer to the next node.

The function 'find_kth_to_last(head, k)' is expected to return the kth to last element of the linked list with 'head' as the head node. If the length of the list is less than 'k', it returns 'None'.

The time complexity of this algorithm is O(n) where n is the length of the list, because we are traversing the list only once. The space complexity is O(1), because we are using a fixed amount of space to store the two pointers.

However, it is important to note that in a real interview, you need to validate the input arguments (e.g., whether the head is 'None' and whether 'k' is non-negative) and discuss edge cases with the interviewer.

5.7 How would you partition a linked list around a value x?

Partitioning a linked list around a value x is a common task. The aim is to rearrange the elements in the list so that all nodes less than x come before all nodes greater than or equal to x.

We can achieve this using following approach:

- Initialize two separate linked lists named 'listSecondsHalf' and 'listFirstHalf', one to store nodes greater than or equal to the value x and the other to store nodes smaller than x.

- Iterate over the original list and add nodes to 'listFirstHalf' and 'listSecondsHalf' list as per their data value.

- Finally, merge 'listFirstHalf' and 'listSecondsHalf'.

Here is the pseudocode for better understanding:

```
function partitionList(head, x):
    listFirstHalf = new LinkedList() # a new linked list
    listSecondHalf = new LinkedList() # another linked list

    node = head # start from the head of the given linked list

    while node != null: # iterate through the original list
        if node.data < x:
            listFirstHalf.add(node.data) # add to the first linked
                list if smaller
        else:
            listSecondHalf.add(node.data) # add to the second linked
                list if larger

        node = node.next # move to the next node

    if listFirstHalf.head == null: # if first list is empty, then
        return the second list
        return listSecondHalf
    elif listSecondHalf.head == null: # if second list is empty,
        then return the first list
        return listFirstHalf

    listFirstHalfTail = getTail(listFirstHalf) # get tail of first
        list
    listFirstHalfTail.next = listSecondHalf.head # connect the first
        list's tail with the second list's head

    return listFirstHalf # return the partitioned list
```

This pseudocode is not language-specific, but it gives an idea about how to approach the problem. In a real coding interview, I would turn this into the language required by the interviewer.

The time complexity of this approach is $O(n)$, where n is the number of nodes in the linked list because you have to traverse the list once to sort the nodes. The space complexity is also $O(n)$ as we are storing the nodes into new linked lists.

It's important to note we maintain the relative ordering of nodes in this approach i.e. nodes with same values keep their original ordering. This hence is a stable algorithm.

5.8 Can you add two numbers represented by linked lists?

To add two numbers represented by linked lists, we need to first understand the properties of linked lists and how the data is represented.

A linked list is a common data structure where elements are nodes that contain two fields: a value and a pointer to the next node. To represent a number with a linked list we use each node to contain a single digit. The number 123 can be represented with a linked list as:

```
1 -> 2 -> 3
```

Let's say we have two numbers represented as linked lists:

```
List1: 7 -> 1 -> 6 represents 617
List2: 5 -> 9 -> 2 represents 295
```

We want to perform the addition:

```
  617
+ 295
-----
  912
```

We can traverse both linked lists and keep adding corresponding nodes into a new linked list which forms the answer. The algorithm would look like this:

1. Initialize current node to dummy head of the returning list.

2. Initialize carry to 0.

3. Loop through lists l1 and l2 until you reach both ends.

- Set the value of l1 to node value if it is not None, else set it to 0.

- Set the value of l2 to node value if it is not None, else set it to 0.

- Calculate sum of values and the carry. If it's above 10, set carry as 1 and reduce sum, if it's not above 10, set carry as 0.

- Create a new node with the digit value of sum and set the next of current node to this new node.

- Advance current node to next.

- Advance both l1 and l2.

4. Check if carry is still left, if so create a new node with digit value of carry.

Here's a Python code snippet that accomplishes this:

```
class Node:
    def __init__(self, data=None):
        self.data = data
        self.next = None

def addTwoLists(first, second):
    # Initialize dummy Node
    res = Node(0);

    # Pointer to store the result
    head = res;

    # To store the carry after
    # summing a node
    carry = 0;

    while(first is not None or second is not None or carry):

        # At the start of each
        # iteration, should be 0
```

```
            # considering there is no
            # number and carry from
            # previous iteration
            sum = 0;

            # If first list is not None
            if(first is not None):
                sum += first.data;
                first = first.next;

            # If second list is not None
            if(second is not None):
                sum+=second.data;
                second = second.next;

            # Add carry from last iteration
            sum += carry;

            # Update carry
            carry = sum // 10;

            # Create a new node with sum
            res.next = Node(sum % 10);

            # Move pointer of resulting list
            res = res.next;

        # if any Nodes left in first list
        if first:
            res.next = first

        # if any Nodes left in second list
        if second:
            res.next = second

        return dummyHead.next
```

This code calculates the sum node by node from both the linked lists, and keeps track of the carry for each calculation. The time complexity of this solution is $O(max(n, m))$ where n and m are the lengths of the two linked lists. This is because we are processing each node from the two linked lists once. The space complexity is also $O(max(n, m))$ as we are allocating space for the new linked list.

5.9 How would you find the intersection point of two linked lists?

Finding the intersection point of two linked lists is a common problem in computer programming interviews. The problem can be solved efficiently using two pointers.

Firstly, let's define the problem: given two linked lists, we need to find the point at which they intersect, or return 'null' if they do not.

1. Brute Force Solution:

The simplest way, though not the most efficient, is to use two nested loops. The outer loop is used for each node of the first linked list and the inner loop compares it with every node of the second linked list. The time complexity for this solution is **O(m*n)**.

2. Hash Table/Map Solution:

By using a hash table or a map, we can store the nodes of one linked list and then check each node of the other linked list to see if it's in the hash table/map or not. However, this method has additional space complexity and takes **O(m + n)** time complexity.

3. Two Pointers Technique Solution:

To solve the problem in an efficient manner (without using additional memory), we would employ a strategy involving two pointers:

(i) Traverse the two linked lists to get their lengths - say 'm' and 'n' for list 1 and list 2 respectively.

(ii) Calculate the difference in lengths 'd = |m - n|'.

(iii) Move the pointer of the larger list 'd' nodes ahead.

(iv) Now traverse both lists simultaneously. When the pointers to the two lists are equal, we have found the intersection.

Here's a Python code snippet showing how to implement it:

```python
def getIntersectionNode(headA, headB):
    lenA, lenB = 0, 0
    tempHeadA, tempHeadB = headA, headB

    while tempHeadA is not None:
        tempHeadA = tempHeadA.next
        lenA += 1

    while tempHeadB is not None:
        tempHeadB = tempHeadB.next
        lenB += 1

    tempHeadA, tempHeadB = headA, headB

    if lenA > lenB:
        for _ in range(lenA - lenB):
            tempHeadA = tempHeadA.next
    else:
        for _ in range(lenB - lenA):
            tempHeadB = tempHeadB.next

    while tempHeadA != tempHeadB:
        tempHeadA = tempHeadA.next
        tempHeadB = tempHeadB.next

    return tempHeadA
```

This algorithm is $O(m + n)$, m and n being the lengths of the two linked lists. This is because we're essentially doing a linear scan of both linked lists to find the lengths and then another linear scan to find the intersection.

The space complexity is $O(1)$, or constant, because we're only using a fixed amount of space to store the pointers and length variables, regardless of the size of the input linked lists.

That's all about finding the intersection point of two linked lists. Note that this problem and its solutions are a good example of how trade-off between time and space complexities can be managed in different situations.

5.10 How would you check if a linked list is a palindrome?

Checking if a linked list is a palindrome involves several steps. Here's a step by step walkthrough.

1. Find the middle of the linked list.

2. Reverse the second half of the linked list.

3. Check if the first half and second half are equal (considering that half denotes the first half if list has odd elements).

4. If they are, then the linked list is a palindrome.

5. Reverse the second half again to restore the original linked list.

For the sake of the explanation, assume the linked list is: [1 -> 2 -> 3 -> 2 -> 1].

1. Find the middle of the linked list

To identify the middle of the linked list, an efficient strategy involves using two pointers, namely 'slow' and 'fast'. Initially, both will point to the head. The 'slow' pointer will move one step at a time, whereas the 'fast' will move two steps. When 'fast' pointer gets to the end, the 'slow' pointer will be in the middle of the list.

Take a look at this Python example:

```python
def find_middle(head):
    slow = head
    fast = head
    while fast is not None and fast.next is not None:
        slow = slow.next
        fast = fast.next.next
    return slow
```

2. Reverse the second half of the linked list

Now, let's create a function 'reverse' which will reverse the order
of the second half of the linked list.

```python
def reverse(second_half):
    prev = None
    while second_half:
        next_node = second_half.next
        second_half.next = prev
        prev = second_half
        second_half = next_node
    return prev
```

3. Check if both halves are equal

Next, we'll compare each node's value in the first half with the
nodes in the reversed second half. If all are identical, the list is
a palindrome.

```python
def is_palindrome(first_half, second_half):
    while second_half:
        if first_half.val != second_half.val:
            return False
        first_half = first_half.next
        second_half = second_half.next
    return True
```

4. Reverse the second half again

Once we have determined if the linked list was a palindrome,
we should restore its original order by reversing the second half
again.

5. The full implementation of the Python function including all steps is:

```python
def is_list_palindrome(head):
    # Step 1: Find middle
    slow = fast = head
    while fast and fast.next:
        slow = slow.next
        fast = fast.next.next

    # Step 2: Reverse second half
    prev = None
    while slow:
        next_node = slow.next
        slow.next = prev
        prev = slow
        slow = next_node
    second_half = prev

    # Step 3: Check palindrome
    while second_half:
        if head.val != second_half.val:
            return False
        head = head.next
        second_half = second_half.next

    return True
```

This algorithm runs in linear time O(N) because we only traverse the linked list a constant number of times. The space complexity is constant, O(1), as we are only using a few extra variables and not any extra space that scales with the input size.

Chapter 6

Stack and Queue Problems

6.1 Can you design a stack with a function that returns the minimum element in constant time?

We can design such a stack using an additional data structure to keep track of the minimum element. We could use an auxiliary stack to just keep track of the minimum element.

The standard operations on a stack are:

1. 'push()' - Adds an element to the top of the stack.
2. 'pop()' – Removes an element from the top of the stack.
3. 'top()' or 'peek()' - Returns the top element of the stack.

4. 'is_empty()' - Checks if the stack is empty.

5. 'size()' – Returns the size of the stack.

But, to this, we are adding another operation 'get_min()' that retrieves the minimum element from the stack in constant time 'O(1)'.

For simplicity, let's say the stack holds integers.

A stack can be implemented using a LinkedList or an Array or a Dynamic Array. Here we will discuss the algorithm which uses two stacks:

We utilize two stacks, 'mainStack' and 'minsStack'. The 'mainStack' holds the actual elements in the stack, while the 'minsStack' holds the minimum elements. The top of 'minsStack' always shows the minimum element from 'mainStack'.

Here is the Python algorithm to implement this:

```python
class MinStack:
    def __init__(self):
        self.mainStack = []
        self.minsStack = []

    # Push operation for adding elements to stack
    def push(self, value):
        self.mainStack.append(value)
        if len(self.minsStack) == 0 or value <= self.minsStack[-1]:
            self.minsStack.append(value)

    # Pop operation for removing elements from stack
    def pop(self):
        if len(self.mainStack) == 0:
            return None
        removed_element = self.mainStack.pop()
        if removed_element == self.minsStack[-1]:
            self.minsStack.pop()
        return removed_element

    # Get Min operation to retrieve minimum element from stack
    def get_min(self):
        if len(self.minsStack) == 0:
            return None
```

```
return self.minsStack[-1]
```

This algorithm ensures all operations ('push()', 'pop()', and 'get_min()') are done in constant time('O(1)'), and it uses 'O(n)' additional space.

Please remember that 'get_min()' does not remove the minimum element – it just returns it.

Regarding mathematical formulas, there is not a lot except for algorithmic time complexity. The crucial part is understanding how two stacks work together to maintain min value, which allows 'get_min()' to always have an 'O(1)' time complexity.

6.2 How would you validate a sequence of pushed and popped elements in a stack?

Stack data structure strictly follows the principle of LIFO (Last In, First Out), which means that the element that is pushed last should be the one to pop first.

Given a sequence of elements that are pushed in a stack and a sequence of elements that are popped, one may need to validate if the popped sequence could have been possibly obtained from the pushed sequence. This problem is largely encountered in a subsection of Stack problems in Data Structures.

Here's how you can validate a sequence of pushed and popped elements in a stack:

The algorithm uses a temporary stack to hold the elements. It iterates the pushed sequence and push the elements into the temporary stack one by one. During each push, it checks if the top element of the stack is equal to the leading elements of the popped sequence.

If the two elements are equal, it pops the top element from the stack, and moves the leading pointer of the popped sequence forward. This process repeats until the top element of the stack is not equal to the leading element of popped sequence.

After iterating the pushed sequence, if there are still elements left in the stack, it checks if the stack elements are popped off in the order of the rest of the popped sequence. If the popped sequences are the same, then the popped sequence is valid, otherwise not.

It is worth noting that if all elements can be popped off from the stack to empty it, it indicates the sequence of popped is valid, otherwise it's invalid.

Here's the Python code that validates a sequence of pushed and popped elements:

```python
def validateStackSequences(pushed, popped):
    j = 0
    stack = []
    for num in pushed:
        stack.append(num)
        while stack and j<len(popped) and stack[-1] == popped[j]:
            stack.pop()
            j += 1

    return j == len(popped)
```

This function takes two parameters: 'pushed' and 'popped', which are list of integers. It returns a boolean value depending on whether the 'popped' sequence is valid or not.

Let's validate the function with the pushed sequence of [1,2,3,4,5] and the popped sequence of [4,5,3,2,1].

```
print(validateStackSequences([1,2,3,4,5], [4,5,3,2,1]))
```

This will output 'True', indicating that the popped sequence [4,5,3,2,1] matches the pushing sequence [1,2,3,4,5].

6.3 Can you implement a queue using stacks?

I can explain how to implement a queue using two stacks in Python. There are two ways two achieve it. The first one is by making 'enqueue' operation costly and the second one is by making 'dequeue' operation costly.

Method 1: Making 'enqueue' operation costly This method makes ensure that the oldest entered element is always at the top of stack 1, so that 'dequeue' operation just pops from stack 1. To put an element at top of stack1, stack 2 is used.

Here is the algorithm:

1. 'Enqueue(q, x)' operation's step are described below:

   - While stack1 is not empty, push everything from satck1 to stack2.
   - Push x to stack1 (assuming size of stacks is unlimited).
   - Push everything back to stack1.

2. 'Dequeue(q)' operation's function are described below:

   - If stack1 is empty then error
   - Pop an item from stack1 and return it

```
class Queue:
    def __init__(self):
        self.s1 = []
        self.s2 = []

    def enqueue(self, x):
        # Move all elements from s1 to s2
        while len(self.s1) != 0:
            self.s2.append(self.s1[-1])
            self.s1.pop()

        # Push item into s1
        self.s1.append(x)

        # Push everything back to s1
        while len(self.s2) != 0:
            self.s1.append(self.s2[-1])
            self.s2.pop()

    def dequeue(self):
        # if first stack is empty
        if len(self.s1) == 0:
            print("Queue is Empty")
        else:
            return self.s1.pop() # pop the first item
```

Method 2: Making 'dequeue' operation costly In this method, in 'enqueue' operation, the new element is entered at the top of stack1. In 'dequeue' operation, if stack2 is empty then all the elements are moved to stack2 and finally top of stack2 is returned.

1. 'Enqueue(q, x)'

- Push x to stack1 (assuming size of stacks is unlimited).

2. 'Dequeue(q)'

- If both stacks are empty then error.

- If stack2 is empty. While stack1 is not empty, push everything from stack1 to stack2.

- Pop the element from stack2 and return it.

Here is the Python code implementing the above idea.

```
class Queue:
    def __init__(self):
        self.s1 = []
        self.s2 = []

    def enqueue(self, x):
        self.s1.append(x)

    def dequeue(self):
        # if first stack is empty
        if len(self.s1) == 0 and len(self.s2) == 0:
            print("Queue is Empty")
        elif len(self.s2) == 0 and len(self.s1) > 0:
            while len(self.s1):
                temp = self.s1.pop()
                self.s2.append(temp)
            return self.s2.pop()
        else:
            return self.s2.pop()
```

We can test this queue implementation as follows:

```
q = Queue()
q.enqueue(1)
q.enqueue(2)
q.enqueue(3)

print(q.dequeue())
print(q.dequeue())
print(q.dequeue())
```

It will output '1 2 3' as expected.

6.4 How would you implement a stack using queues?

A stack can be implemented using two queues. Here's how you can implement the push and pop operations of a stack:

1. Push operation: For every pushed element, we remove all elements from 'queue1' and append them to 'queue2', then add

the pushed element in 'queue1' and finally add back all elements from 'queue2' to 'queue1'. So, after any push operation, 'queue1' will always contain the full stack so that its head is the top of the stack.

Here's a Python implementation of the 'push' operation:

```
def push(x):
    # Pushing x to queue1
    queue1.append(x)

    # Pushing the rest of the elements in queue1 into queue2
    for _ in range(len(queue1)-1):
        queue1.append(queue1.pop(0))
```

2. Pop operation: As we maintained the condition where the head of 'queue1' is always the top of the stack, 'pop()' operation is as simple as dequeuing from 'queue1'.

Here's the Python implementation of the 'pop' operation:

```
def pop():
    # if first queue is empty
    if len(queue1) == 0:
        print("Stack is Empty.")
        return
    return queue1.pop(0)
```

Here's a visual representation of the process:

```
For instance, suppose we're pushing 1, 2, and 3 in this order:

Initially: queue1=[]

Push 1: queue1=[1]

Push 2: queue2=[1], queu1=[2], queue1=[2,1]

Push 3: queue2=[2,1], queue1=[3], queue1=[3,2,1]

So in this case, to get the top of the stack (3), we just return the
   front of queue1. To pop, we simply dequeue from queue1.
```

You must note that this method makes the 'push' operation

more costly. The 'push' operation takes $O(n)$ time as it involves reversing 'queue1' with helping of 'queue2'. Meanwhile, the 'pop' operation only takes $O(1)$ time. If you want to make the 'push' operation less costly, you might want to reverse the roles of 'queue1' and 'queue2' in the 'push' and 'pop' operations.

Also note that the above implementation is not thread safe. If multiple threads execute operations on the stack at the same time, the behavior might violate the Stack data structure's contract.

6.5   Can you sort a stack in ascending order (with biggest items on top)?

You can sort a stack in ascending order (with biggest items on top) using another temporary stack. The idea of the sorting algorithm is to pull an item from the original stack and push it on the other stack. If pushing this item would violate the sort order of the new stack, you need to remove enough items from it and push them back on the original stack before pushing the new item. The popped elements from the temporary stack which are greater than the element to be inserted are kept in recursion and then we call insert to insert the new element in the temporary (or auxiliary) stack in its rightful place.

Here's the algorithm in detail:

1. Create an empty 'auxiliary' stack.

2. While the original stack is not empty:

- Pop an element from the original stack, call it 'temp'.

- While the 'auxiliary' stack is not empty and the top of the 'auxiliary' stack is less than 'temp', pop from 'auxiliary' and push back to the original stack. Repeat this step until the condition is false.

- Push 'temp' into 'auxiliary'.

3. The 'auxiliary' stack now contains the original stack's elements sorted such that the largest element is at the top of the stack.

Here is the pseudo-code for the above algorithm:

```
def sortedInsert(s, element):
    if len(s) == 0 or element > s[-1]:
        s.append(element)
        return
    temp = s.pop()
    sortedInsert(s, element)
    s.append(temp)

def sortStack(s):
    if len(s)!= 0:
        temp = s.pop()
        sortStack(s)
        sortedInsert(s, temp)

# main
s = []
s.append(3)
s.append(5)
s.append(1)
s.append(4)
s.append(2)
sortStack(s)
```

In above pseudo-code, sortStack function is a recursive function and sortedInsert function is also a recursive function used to insert the popped items back to the 'auxiliary' stack ('s' in this case) at correct positions.

This algorithm has a time complexity of $O(n^2)$. For each element, it's popped once from the original stack and then pushed once in the 'auxiliary' stack. For every insertion, we may pop from 'auxiliary' stack and push it back up to n times. Hence the total time complexity is $O(n)$ for pop and push operations and $O(n^2)$ for insert operation and hence $O(n^2)$ in total.

6.6 How would you design a call center with three levels of employees: operator, supervisor, and director using queues?

The task can be accomplished using a priority queue where elements are sorted based on their importance in ascending or descending order.

The priority queue is a data structure that is very similar to a queue and it is used to manage data that has been assigned a priority. In a priority queue, items with higher priority get ahead of items with lower priority or based on the sequence data arrived. Priorities could be both i.e. in increasing and decreasing order.

Levels Of Employees:

- Operator (Level - 1)
- Supervisor (Level - 2)
- Director (Level - 3)

In the scenario you described, the problem sounds like it might be best modeled by multiple queues, one for each role, rather than a single priority queue. We could pull calls off of the different queues based on the priority of the role. The operators would promise to offload as many calls as possible through a round-robin from their queue, followed by the supervisors, and then the directors if necessary.

Operator

They will handle the calls first.

$$Q_{op} = \{c_1, c_2, c_3, \ldots, c_n\} \tag{6.1}$$

Where Q_{op} denotes the queue of operators and c_i are the calls waiting in the queue.

Supervisor

If all operators are busy, the call goes to Supervisor.

$$Q_{sp} = \{c_{n+1}, c_{n+2}, c_{n+3}, \ldots, c_{2n}\} \tag{6.2}$$

Where Q_{sp} denotes the queue of supervisors.

Director

If all operators and supervisors are busy, the call goes to Director.

$$Q_{dir} = \{c_{2n+1}, c_{2n+2}, c_{2n+3}, \ldots, c_{3n}\} \tag{6.3}$$

Where Q_{dir} denotes the queue of directors.

Algorithm

Here is a pseudo-code that describes the logic of the call-handling process:

```
while (incoming_calls):
  if not queue_operators.is_empty():
    assign_call(queue_operators.dequeue())
  elif not queue_supervisors.is_empty():
    assign_call(queue_supervisors.dequeue())
  elif not queue_directors.is_empty():
    assign_call(queue_directors.dequeue())
  else:
    # Make the call wait in a queue
    wait_queue.enqueue(incoming_call)
```

Here, 'assign_call()' is a function to assign the call to the respective employee. And, 'enqueue()' and 'dequeue()' are basic queue operations to insert an element into the queue and remove an element from the queue respectively.

This way, every incoming call will be directly assigned to an operator unless all operators are busy. The call will be then escalated to the supervisor if all operators are currently busy. If supervisors are also busy, then it will be escalated to directors.

If all three levels are busy at the moment, the incoming calls will wait in a separate queue until they get a free slot from any of the three levels (i.e., Operator, Supervisor, and Director).

The model assumes calls are serviced one by one, and the hierarchy is strict, i.e., an available supervisor won't pick a call if there is any operator free. This guarantees that calls are handled at the lower level possible.

This model can be enhanced by time slicing or allowing higher levels to pick calls if they have been idle for too long, but those details depend on the business rules of the call center.

6.7   Can you solve the Tower of Hanoi problem using stacks?

The Tower of Hanoi puzzle is a classical problem of recursion and can indeed be solved using stacks in the context of computer programming.

The Tower of Hanoi problem is a puzzle that involves moving n discs of different sizes from one rod to another, using a certain set of rules:

1. Only one disk can be moved at a time.

2. A disk can only be moved if it is the uppermost disk on a stack.

3. No disk may be placed on top of a smaller disk.

To solve it using stacks, you can exploit the simple fact that a stack of disks in descending order (largest disk at the bottom, smallest at the top) represents a valid state of a Hanoi rod.

Assuming you have three rods (or three stacks), namely source, auxiliary, and destination, here's how you would solve it:

1. Move n-1 disks from the source to the auxiliary rod (using the destination as the temporary rod).

2. Move the nth disk from the source to the destination rod.

3. Move the n-1 disks from the auxiliary rod to the destination rod (using the source rod as the temporary rod).

Given this, a possible Python solution using stacks could look like this:

```python
def hanoi(n, source, destination, auxiliary):
    if n > 0:
        # Move n - 1 disks from source to auxiliary, so they are out
```

```
        of the way
    hanoi(n - 1, source, auxiliary, destination)

    # Move the nth disk from source to destination
    destination.append(source.pop())

    # Move the n - 1 disks that we left on auxiliary to
        destination
    hanoi(n - 1, auxiliary, destination, source)
# Initiate call from source rod to destination rod with auxiliary
    rod
source = [3, 2, 1]
destination = []
auxiliary = []
hanoi(len(source), source, destination, auxiliary)
```

In this example, "source", "destination" and "auxiliary" are all stacks that simulate the rods in the problem. Initially, all disks are on the "source" rod. After calling hanoi, all disks end up on the "destination" rid, obeying the rules of the puzzle.

Just remember that this is a recursive function and it solves this problem in $O(2^n)$ time complexity, where n is the number of disks. This isn't the most efficient solution in terms of time complexity, but the Tower of Hanoi problem is a classic example of a problem where the solution naturally fits a recursive algorithmic approach based on the problem's rules.

6.8   How would you implement a circular queue?

A Circular Queue (also known as a Ring Buffer) is a linear data structure that follows the First In First Out (FIFO) principle. In a typical queue data structure, we cannot reuse the spaces once an element is removed. However, the circular queue modulates the end of the queue to the beginning, allowing continuous reusability of the queue.

Here's a simple implementation of a circular queue in Python.
Our queue consists of an array 'queue' and two integers, 'front'
and 'rear'. The array holds the items in the queue, while 'front'
and 'rear' represent indices of the starting and end points in
the queue.

```python
class CircularQueue:
    def __init__(self, k):
        self.k = k
        self.queue = [None] * k
        self.front = self.rear = -1

    # Insert an element at the rear
    def enQueue(self, data):
        if ((self.rear + 1) % self.k == self.front):
            print("Circular Queue is fulln")

        elif (self.front == -1):
            self.front = 0
            self.rear = 0
            self.queue[self.rear] = data
        else:
            self.rear = (self.rear + 1) % self.k
            self.queue[self.rear] = data

    # Remove element from the front
    def deQueue(self):
        if (self.front == -1):
            print("Circular Queue is emptyn")

        elif (self.front == self.rear):
            temp=self.queue[self.front]
            self.front = -1
            self.rear = -1
            return temp
        else:
            temp = self.queue[self.front]
            self.front = (self.front + 1) % self.k
            return temp

    # Display the queue
    def display(self):
        if(self.front == -1):
            print("No element in the Circular Queue")

        elif (self.rear >= self.front):
            for i in range(self.front, self.rear + 1):
                print(self.queue[i], end = " ")
        else:
            for i in range(self.front, self.k):
```

```
    print(self.queue[i], end = "␣")
for i in range(0, self.rear + 1):
    print(self.queue[i], end = "␣")
```

In the 'enQueue' operation, we check:

- If the queue is full '(self.rear + 1)

- If it's empty, then the front and rear are at the same location.

- Otherwise, we move the rear to the next position '(self.rear + 1)

In the 'deQueue' operation, we check:

- If the queue is empty '(self.front == -1)'.

- If the front and rear are at the same location, then we make the queue empty after the 'deQueue' operation.

- Otherwise, we move the front to the next position '(self.front + 1)

In the 'display' operation, we handle the case when the rear has wrapped to an index before front. We display elements from front to the end of array and then from start to rear.

6.9 Can you reverse a stack without using any additional data structures?

While there are numerous ways to solve this problem, given the constraint you've outlined — not using any additional data structures — we should solve it using recursion. The reason for this is because, even though it may not be entirely obvious at first, recursion has a built-in stack!

Here's the general pseudocode:

1. Use the technique of removing all items from the stack recursively until it is empty.

2. While popping items off the stack in this recursive process, instead of immediately reinserting an item after removing it, delay this step until the stack is fully empty.

3. Then, insert all items back into it. The last item we pop off will be the first one we push back in, and so forth, effectively reversing the stack.

If you think about it long enough, this is akin to using an additional stack, but formally speaking, it's completely void of any additional data structures.

Here's the actual code for this process, in Python:

```python
def insert_at_bottom(stack, item):
    if len(stack) == 0:
        stack.append(item)
    else:
        temp = stack.pop()
        insert_at_bottom(stack, item)
        stack.append(temp)


def reverse_stack(stack):
    if len(stack) > 0:
        temp = stack.pop()
        reverse_stack(stack)
        insert_at_bottom(stack, temp)
```

You first define a helper function, 'insert_at_bottom', to place an item at the bottom of the stack. You then define your main function, 'reverse_stack', which uses this helper to reverse the stack.

The function 'reverse_stack' pops an item from the stack and calls itself to reverse the remaining items. Once that is achieved (the remaining stack is empty), it uses 'insert_at_bottom' to place the popped items back but at the bottom of the stack.

This results in the stack being reversed.

However, It's important to note that this method might not be the most efficient one for large data sets and could potentially cause a stack overflow error due to high recursion depth especially in languages that have small maximum recursion depth like Python.

6.10   Can you design a priority queue?

A priority queue is a special type of queue in which each element is associated with a priority and is served according to its priority level. If elements with the same priority occur, they are served according to their order in the queue.

Here's a design for a basic priority queue using a binary heap. Keep in mind that there are several possible ways to implement a priority queue, and the best method depends on the specific requirements of your problem. This method has an average time complexity of O(log n) for insertions and deletions, and O(n) for building the initial queue from an array of items.

Here's the priority queue class:

```python
class PriorityQueue:
    def __init__(self):
        self.heap = []

    def is_empty(self):
        return len(self.heap) == 0

    def push(self, priority, item):
        heapq.heappush(self.heap, (priority, item))

    def pop(self):
        _, item = heapq.heappop(self.heap)
        return item
```

```
def peek(self):
    return self.heap[0][1]
```

In this class, 'push' method inserts an item into the queue by appending it to end and reorders the heap to maintain the heap property. 'pop' method deletes the root from the heap, reorders the heap, and returns the item associated with the previous root. 'peek' method gives the highest priority element but does not modify the heap.

This PriorityQueue class is a binary min heap - the parent node is less than or equal to its children. An element with high priority is considered to have low value and is therefore given precedence.

Now, you want to use it:

```
priority_queue = PriorityQueue()

# inserting elements into the priority queue
priority_queue.push(3, "Apple")
priority_queue.push(1, "Banana")
priority_queue.push(2, "Cherry")

# removing elements from the priority queue
print(priority_queue.pop()) # Outputs: Banana
print(priority_queue.pop()) # Outputs: Cherry
print(priority_queue.pop()) # Outputs: Apple
```

Here, the elements are served according to their priority. Since 1 has the highest priority, "Banana" is served first, then "Cherry" with the second highest priority (2), and finally "Apple" with the lowest priority (3).

This example follows Python's standard library 'heapq' which provides functions for creating min heap. If you want to create a max heap, you can simply invert the values or priorities.

And, as always, it's good to add error checking in production-level code (for example, checking that the queue isn't empty before popping).

This structure can be visualized in the form of a binary tree or a heap tree for better understanding.

If you want more advanced features like searching for or removing arbitrary elements, you could use a more complex data structure such as a balanced binary search tree or a Fibonacci heap. But these are much more complex to implement and understand, and typically have slower average-case performance for a basic priority queue.

Chapter 7

Tree and Graph Problems

7.1 How would you determine if a binary tree is balanced?

Balancing a binary tree often refers to ensuring that the depth of the left and right subtrees of every node differs by at most 1.

To determine if a binary tree is balanced, you could use a depth-first search (DFS) strategy. To implement this, you'll post-order traverse through the tree. For each node, you compute the heights of its left and right subtrees. If the difference in heights is more than 1, then the tree is not balanced.

Here's the pseudocode of this approach:

```
define function isBalanced(tree) {
```

```
    return (height(tree) != -1)
}

define function height(node) {
  if (is_empty(node)) {
    return 0
  }

  leftHeight = height(node.left)
  if (leftHeight == -1){
    return -1
  }

  rightHeight = height(node.right)
  if (rightHeight == -1) {
    return -1
  }

  if (abs(leftHeight - rightHeight) > 1) {
    return -1
  } else {
    return max(leftHeight, rightHeight) + 1
  }
}
```

The 'height' function returns -1 if the tree is unbalanced. In-side the 'isBalanced' function, we check if the height function returns -1. If it returns -1, then the tree is unbalanced, and the 'isBalanced' function returns False. If the height function doesn't return -1, then the tree is balanced, and the 'isBalanced' function returns True.

Finally, note that in the worst-case scenario, this algorithm has to traverse through all nodes of the tree, so its time complexity is $O(n)$, where n is the number of nodes in the tree. This is the most efficient approach for this problem since any algorithm will have to visit all nodes at least once.

Note: This code assumes that an empty tree is balanced and that the height of an empty tree is 0. In some contexts, this may not be the desired definition. Be sure to clarify these points with your interviewer.

7.2 Can you implement a Breadth-First Search on a graph?

Breadth-First Search (BFS) is an algorithm used for traversing or searching tree or graph data structures. It starts from a selected node (source or root) and traverses the graph layerwise, exploring the neighbour nodes (ie, nodes which are directly connected to source node). It then moves towards the next-level neighbors.

Here's a Python algorithm for BFS:

```python
def bfs(graph, root):
    visited, queue = set(), collections.deque([root])
    visited.add(root)

    while queue:

        # Dequeue a vertex from queue
        vertex = queue.popleft()
        print(str(vertex) + "␣", end="")

        # If not visited, marked it as visited and enqueue it
        for neighbour in graph[vertex]:
            if neighbour not in visited:
                visited.add(neighbour)
                queue.append(neighbour)
```

The 'bfs' function takes in a graph and a starting node (root) as parameters. The graph is a dictionary of lists where the dictionary keys are the graph vertices, and the list in each key contains the vertices that are adjacent to the key.

Here is an example of using BFS in a graph:

```python
# Construct the graph
graph = {
  'A' : ['B','C'],
  'B' : ['D', 'E'],
  'C' : ['F'],
  'D' : [],
  'E' : ['F'],
```

```
   'F' : []
 }

 bfs(graph, 'A') # Output: A B C D E F
```

In the above example, we start traversing from 'A'. 'A' has two
adjacent nodes: 'B' and 'C'. After visiting them, we visit the
neighbours of 'B' which are 'D' and 'E'. 'D' does not have any
neighbors and 'E' has one neighbor 'F'. Finally, we visit 'F'.

The time complexity of BFS can be obtained by following reasoning:

- Each vertex is processed once as BFS ensures that a vertex is not
processed more than once.

- Each edge is also processed once.

Thus, the overall time complexity is $O(V + E)$, where:

- V is the number of vertices

- E is the number of edges in the graph.

The space complexity of BFS is $O(V)$, as it needs to store the
vertices in the queue. Here, V is the number of vertices in a
graph.

7.3   How would you implement a Depth-First Search on a graph?

Depth-first search (DFS) is an algorithm for traversing or searching tree or graph data structures. Starting at the root (in case
of a tree) or an arbitrary node (in case of a graph), the algorithm explores as far as possible along each branch before

backtracking.

Here is a high-level DFS algorithm:

```
DFS(node):
  if node is visited:
    return
  mark node as visited
  for each neighbor of node:
    DFS(neighbor)
```

To implement DFS, we typically use a stack data structure.

Here's some pseudo-code that implements DFS with a stack to track the traversal:

```
DFS-iterative(node):
  create a stack S and push node into it
  mark node as visited
  while S is not empty:
    v = S.pop()        # Pop a vertex from stack to visit next
    visit(v)
    for each neighbor x of v:
      if x is not visited:
        push x into S
        mark x as visited
```

We assume the presence of a helper function 'visit(v)', which handles the logic to be performed when visiting node 'v'.

Let's take an example graph:

```
{1: [2, 3], 2: [4, 5], 3: [], 4: [], 5: []}
```

This can be visualized as:

```
1
/ \
2   3
/ \
4   5
```

If we start our DFS from node 1, the order of traversal will be

'1-2-4-5-3'.

To improve this pseudo-code, you would also typically create a 'Node' object that has a 'visited' field, rather than marking them as visited externally.

It's also worth noting that in terms of time complexity, DFS takes $O(V + E)$ time, where V is the number of vertices and E is the number of edges, because every vertex and every edge will be explored in the worst case. DFS takes $O(V)$ space, due to the storage required for the stack and the visited map.

Please note that this is a high level overview of DFS and, depending on the specifics of your graph and the problem at hand, you might need to adapt it.

Unfortunately, charts and mathematical formulas are not typically used in the explanation of Depth-First Search implementation, because it is primarily a procedural concept and therefore can best be described in the form of these procedural pseudo-code.

7.4 Can you find the lowest common ancestor of two nodes in a binary tree?

The Lowest Common Ancestor (LCA) in a binary tree for two nodes 'n1' and 'n2' is the deepest (lowest) node 'v' that is an ancestor of both 'n1' and 'n2'. If we designate each move from a node to its parent as a step, 'v' would be the node for which the sum of the distances from 'v' to 'n1' and 'n2' is the smallest. Here is the procedure to find the LCA in a binary tree:

First, we need to traverse the tree starting from the root node and search for nodes 'n1' and 'n2' (this can be completed using depth-first search, also known as DFS). For the DFS traversal, we can use a stack-based iterative method or a recursion-based approach.

Each time we visit a node during the DFS traversal, we record its parent. The parent can be stored in a dictionary.

Then, we create a set to contain all the ancestors for 'n1' by exploring up from 'n1' to root in the parent dictionary.

After that, we travel up from 'n2' to the root. The first node that appears in the 'n1''s ancestor set we have collected earlier will be the LCA. If 'n2' reaches the root first, then 'n2' will be the LCA.

Now let's break the algorithm into pseudocode:

```
def findLCA(root, n1, n2):
    parent = {root: None}
    stack = [root]

    # Step 1: DFS until we find both the nodes n1 and n2
    while n1 not in parent or n2 not in parent:
        node = stack.pop()
        if node.left:
            parent[node.left] = node
            stack.append(node.left)
        if node.right:
            parent[node.right] = node
            stack.append(node.right)

    # Step 2: Create a set of n1's ancestors
    ancestors = set()
    while n1:
        ancestors.add(n1)
        n1 = parent[n1]

    # Step 3: The first ancestor of n2 which appears in
    # n1's ancestor set() is their lowest common ancestor
    while n2 not in ancestors:
        n2 = parent[n2]

    return n2
```

Note: An important thing to mention about this code is that for it to work as is, it assumes that nodes 'n1' and 'n2' are guaranteed to be in the tree. If that's not the case, the code should be modified to handle the scenario when 'n1' and/or 'n2' are not in the tree. Also, since binary trees do not have a parent pointer, this code creates an additional data structure, a map to track parent pointers. If you have a binary tree with parent pointer or if you can modify the node structure to include a parent pointer, you can take advantage of this simplification.

This algorithm runs in 'O(N)' time where 'N' is the number of nodes in the binary tree (due to the DFS) and requires 'O(N)' space to keep track of parent pointers.

7.5   How would you check if a graph is a tree?

A graph is a tree if it is connected and doesn't have a cycle. To formally define these terms:

- A graph is connected if there's a path between every pair of vertices.

- A graph has a cycle if there's a non-empty trail in which the start and end vertices are the same.

So we can implement the following algorithm to check, if a graph is a tree:

1. Check if there is a cycle in the provided graph

2. If there is a cycle, the graph is not a tree.

3. If there is no cycle, check if the graph is connected.

4. If the graph is connected, it is a tree.

Here are the details of each step:

1. **Checking for Cycle** - Depth First Traversal can be used to detect a cycle in a Graph. DFS for a connected graph produces a tree. There is a cycle in a graph only if there is a back edge present in the graph. A back edge is an edge that is joining a node to itself (self-loop) or one of its ancestors in the tree produced by DFS. You can use the below pseudo-code to detect cycle:

```
def isCyclicUtil(v, visited, parent):

    visited[v] = True

    for i in graph[v]:

        if visited[i] == False:
            if isCyclicUtil(i, visited, v) == True:
                return True
        elif parent != i:
            return True

    return False

def isCyclic():

    visited =[False]*(len(graph))

    for i in range(len(graph)):
        if visited[i] == False:
            if isCyclicUtil(i, visited, -1) == True:
                return True

    return False
```

2. **Checking for connected graph** - While doing DFS traversal mark every visited vertex, if we get any vertex which is not visited, means graph is not connected.

```
def DFS(v, visited):

    visited[v] = True

    for i in graph[v]:
        if visited[i] == False:
            DFS(i, visited)

def isConnected():
```

```
visited =[False]*(len(graph))

DFS(0, visited)

for i in range(len(graph)):
    if visited[i] == False:
        return False

return True
```

The graph is a tree if it passes both these checks.

The time complexity for both these operations is O(V+E) where V is the number of vertices in the graph and E is the number of edges since we are using DFS traversal.

7.6   Can you find the shortest path between two nodes in a graph?

One of the most common and effective methods for finding the shortest path in a graph is Dijkstra's Algorithm.

Dijkstra's Algorithm works by visiting vertices in the graph starting from the object's starting point. It then repeatedly selects the unvisited vertex with the lowest distance, calculates the distance through it to each unvisited neighbor, and updates the neighbor's distance if smaller. Mark visited (set to red) when done with neighbors.

Here is a step by step breakdown of Dijkstra's algorithm using pseudo code:

1. Create a set (sptSet) that will contain all the vertices included in the shortest path tree i.e., the shortest distance from

the source vertex to the vertex has been finalized. 2. Initialize distance values as:

- Distance of source vertex from itself is always 0.

$$d[source] = 0$$

- Distance of all other vertices from the starting point is set to infinity initially.

$$d[v] = \qquad v \neq source$$

3. Until sptSet includes all vertices, follow the subsequent steps:

- Pick any vertex 'u' that isn't contained within the sptSet and has a minimum distance-value index.

- Include 'u' to the sptSet.

- Based on the current node, update distance values of all adjacent vertices of picked vertex 'u'. For every adjacent vertex 'v', if the sum of distance value of 'u' from source and the weight of edge 'u-v' is less than the distance value of 'v', then update the distance value of 'v'.

The formula to update the adjacent vertices is: if $d[u]+cost_{u,v} < d[v]$ then update $d[v] = d[u] + cost_{u,v}$

Let's take an example of the following graph:

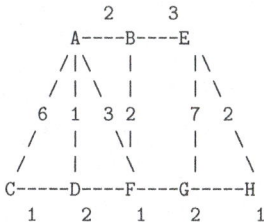

```
      2    3
    A----B----E
   /|\   |    |\
  / | \  |    | \
 6  1  3 2    7  2
 /  |   \|    |   \
/   |    \    |    \
C-----D----F----G-----H
1    2    1    2     1
```

The shortest path from vertex 'A' to 'H' is A->B->E->H with cost=2+3+2=7.

Dijkstra's Algorithm has a time complexity of $O(V^2)$ (for adjacency matrix representation of a graph) where 'V' is the number of vertices. However, using binary heap, time complexity can be reduced to 'O(E log V)', where 'E' is the number of edges.

You might want to use Dijkstra's algorithm if, for example, you are building a software for a GPS, and you need to calculate the quickest route from one place to another.

However, It's worth noting that Dijkstra's Algorithm doesn't work with graphs that contain negative weight edges. For graphs with negative weight edges, one can use Bellman–Ford algorithm.

7.7 How would you convert a binary search tree to a doubly-linked list?

Converting a binary search tree (BST) into a doubly-linked list involves an in-order traversal of the BST and properly adjusting the right and left pointers of each node so that they follow the doubly-linked list properties.

Let's define the process with a recursive function.

```
def flatten(root):
    if root is None:
        return None

    # Initially, both lists are empty
    head, tail = None, None

    # Recursively convert the left sub-tree
    if root.left is not None:
```

```
        head, tail = flatten(root.left)

        # Make right pointer of tail node point to root
        tail.right = root
        # Make left pointer of root point to tail
        root.left = tail

    # If left sub-tree is empty, the head is root
    if head is None:
        head = root

    # Save the node into tail which is needed when right sub-tree is
         empty
    temp = root

    # Recursively convert the right sub-tree
    if root.right is not None:
        temp, tail = flatten(root.right)

        # Make left pointer of first node of result point to root
        temp.left = root
        # Make right pointer of root point to the first node of right
             sub-tree
        root.right = temp

    # If right sub-tree is empty, the tail is root
    if tail is None:
        tail = root

    return head, tail
```

Here, 'flatten()' function takes a root of a BST and returns the head and tail of the doubly linked list. It first checks if the root is 'None' and returns 'None' in this case. Then, it initializes 'head' and 'tail' as 'None'.

It recursively flattens the left sub-tree and if the root's left is not 'None', it makes the right pointer of tail node point to root and makes left pointer of the root point to tail. If the root's left is 'None', 'head' is root.

It saves the current root into 'temp' which is needed when the right sub-tree is empty.

Similarly, it recursively flattens the right sub-tree and if the root's right is not 'None', it makes the left pointer of first node of right sub-tree point to root and makes the right pointer of

root point to the first node of the right sub-tree. If the root's
right is 'None', 'tail' is root.

Finally, it returns the 'head' and 'tail'.

For example, if the BST is:

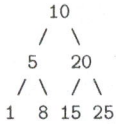

```
    10
   /  \
  5    20
 / \  / \
1   8 15 25
```

Then, the DLL will be:

```
1 <-> 5 <-> 8 <-> 10 <-> 15 <-> 20 <-> 25
```

7.8 How would you find the diameter of a binary tree?

The diameter of a binary tree refers to the longest path between
any two nodes in a binary tree. This path may or may not pass
through the root.

Algorithm to find the diameter of a binary tree:

1. Compute the height (or depth) of the left subtree.

2. Compute the height of the right subtree.

3. Compute the diameter of the left subtree.

4. Compute the diameter of the right subtree.

5. Return the maximum value of the following three:

* The diameter of the left subtree.

* The diameter of the right subtree.

* The sum of the height of the left subtree and the height of the right subtree. (This corresponds to the longest path through the root)

We can implement this algorithm using a simple recursive function in any programming language.

In Python, for example, you might write a function like this:

```python
class Node:
    def __init__(self, data):
        self.data = data
        self.left = None
        self.right = None


def height(node):
    if node is None:
        return 0
    return 1 + max(height(node.left), height(node.right))


def diameter(node):
    if node is None:
        return 0

    lheight = height(node.left)
    rheight = height(node.right)

    ldiameter = diameter(node.left)
    rdiameter = diameter(node.right)

    return max(lheight + rheight + 1, max(ldiameter, rdiameter))


# Testing the function
root = Node(1)
root.left = Node(2)
root.right = Node(3)
root.left.left = Node(4)
root.left.right = Node(5)

print("Diameter of the given binary tree is %d" % (diameter(root)))
```

The time complexity of the above function is $O(N^2)$ and since we're computing the height in every recursive call, we can optimize the function by calculating the height in the same recursive function where we're calculating the diameter of the tree.

To implement this, we can make the function to return two values: the height and the diameter of the node as a pair or struct depending on the programming language you're using.

Here's how you might change the function in Python:

```python
class Node(object):
    def __init__(self, value):
        self.value = value
        self.left = None
        self.right = None

def diameter_of_binary_tree(root):
    diameter, _ = get_diameter_and_height(root)
    return diameter

def get_diameter_and_height(node):
    if node is None:
        return 0, 0

    ld, lh = get_diameter_and_height(node.left)
    rd, rh = get_diameter_and_height(node.right)

    return max(lh + rh, ld, rd), 1 + max(lh, rh)
# Testing the function
root = Node(1)
root.left = Node(2)
root.right = Node(3)
root.left.left = Node(4)
root.left.right = Node(5)

print("Diameter of the binary tree is %d" % (diameter_of_binary_tree
    (root)))
```

So there is your optimized Python solution.

The time complexity of this optimized method is O(N), where N is the number of nodes in the binary tree. This is because we're visiting every node once.

The space complexity is $O(\log N)$ for a balanced tree and $O(N)$ in the worst case, due to recursion. This represents the maximum number of concurrent recursive function calls that we have at any one point - i.e., the maximum depth of the recursion.

7.9 Can you print the boundary of a binary tree?

We can print the boundary of a binary tree. Here's a step-by-step approach to solving this:

A Binary Tree boundary is defined as the perimeter of the binary tree. Starting from the root, boundary traversal should be done anti-clockwise starting from the root. Boundary includes left boundary, leaves, and right boundary.

To print the boundary, we divide the problem in three parts:

1. Print the left boundary in top-down manner.

2. Print all leaf nodes from left to right, which can again be sub-divided into two sub-parts:

  2.1 Print all leaf nodes of the left sub-tree from left to right.

  2.2 Print all leaf nodes of the right subtree from left to right.

3. Print the right boundary in bottom-up manner.

We need to take care of one thing that nodes are not printed again. For example, the left most node is also the leaf node of the tree.

Here is the pseudocode to implement the above approach:

```
# A function to print all left boundary nodes, except a leaf node.
def printLeftBoundary(node):
    if node:
        if node.left:
            # to ensure top-down order, print the node
            # before calling itself for left subtree
            print(node.data)
            printLeftBoundary(node.left)
        elif node.right:
            print(node.data)
            printLeftBoundary(node.right)
        # do nothing if it is a leaf node, this way we avoid
        # duplicates in output

# A function to print all right boundary nodes, except a leaf node
def printRightBoundary(node):
    if node:
        if node.right:
            # to ensure bottom-up order, first call for right
            # subtree, then print this node
            printRightBoundary(node.right)
            print(node.data)
        elif node.left:
            printRightBoundary(node.left)
            print(node.data)

# A function to print all leaf nodes
def printLeaves(node):
    if node:
        printLeaves(node.left)
        # print it if it is a leaf node
        if node.left is None and node.right is None:
            print(node.data)
        printLeaves(node.right)

# A function to do boundary traversal of a given binary tree
def printBoundary(node):
    if node:
        print(node.data)
        # Print the left boundary in top-down manner
        printLeftBoundary(node.left)
        # Print all leaf nodes
        printLeaves(node.left)
        printLeaves(node.right)
        # Print the right boundary in bottom-up manner
        printRightBoundary(node.right)
```

Note, this technique works best with binary trees, not binary search trees (BSTs). In binary search trees, data is organized in a specific way that can be leveraged for more efficient solutions. However, with binary trees, data is relatively unorganized and requires a more comprehensive traversal and printing technique.

7.10   How would you serialize and deserialize a binary tree?

Serializing a binary tree involves converting the binary tree into a string representation that can be easily stored or transmitted. Deserializing involves reconstructing the tree from the stored string representation. For this example, let's define a binary tree node as follows:

```
class Node:
    def __init__(self, x):
        self.val = x
        self.left = None
        self.right = None
```

Serialization

One common way to do this is to perform a depth-first pre-order traversal of the original tree, converting each node's value into a string on the go.

```
def serialize(self, root):
    """Encodes a tree to a single string.

        :type root: TreeNode
        :rtype: str
    """
    if root is None:
        return 'None,'
    return str(root.val) + ',' + self.serialize(root.left) + self.serialize(root.right)
```

The function 'serialize' is recursive. Notice that if the node is None (leaf node), it returns 'None,'. This is useful for identifying leaf nodes during deserialisation.

Deserialization

To deserialize, we'll break the string apart with ',' as the delimiter. When constructing the binary tree, we'll remove values from the list and traverse the tree in the same pre-order that we used when serializing.

Here's the code:

```python
def deserialize(self, data):
    """Decodes your encoded data to tree.

    :type data: str
    :rtype: TreeNode
    """
    def helper(data_list):
        if data_list[0] == 'None':
            data_list.pop(0)
            return None
        node = Node(int(data_list[0]))
        data_list.pop(0)
        node.left = helper(data_list)
        node.right = helper(data_list)
        return node

    data_list = data.split(',')
    return helper(data_list)
```

The function 'helper' is recursive. It pops the first element from 'data_list' and uses that to create a new TreeNode 'node', does the same for 'node.left' and 'node.right', and finally returns 'node'.

In this method, the time complexity is O(n) for both serialization and deserialization, where n is the number of nodes. This is because we visit each node exactly once. The space complexity is also O(n) because in the worst case (i.e., the tree is completely unbalanced, like a linked list), the call stack could be n layers deep.

Chapter 8

Recursion and Dynamic Programming Problems

8.1 Can you write a recursive function to compute the Fibonacci sequence?

One of the common examples of recursion in programming is computing the Fibonacci sequence. In Python, it can be realized like below:

```python
def fibonacci(n):
    if n <= 0:
        return "Input should be a positive integer"
    elif n == 1:
        return 0
    elif n == 2:
        return 1
    else:
        return fibonacci(n-1) + fibonacci(n-2)
```

The above function calculates the Fibonacci sequence utilising the nature of the Fibonacci sequence, where each number in the sequence is the sum of the two preceding ones (considering that $F(0) = 0$, and $F(1) = 1$). Hence, the term 'fibonacci(n) = fibonacci(n-1) + fibonacci(n-2)'.

Now, the recursive call happens with 'fibonacci(n-1)' and 'fibonacci(n-2)', but what are they? They are essentially tasks that are a version of the original computation 'fibonacci(n)' but on simpler inputs. Here, values decrease with 'n-1' and 'n-2'. The function will keep calling itself, decreasing the input on each call, until it reaches a base case.

Recursion always needs a base case — the situation where the function does not call itself — to avoid infinite recursion. In this case, it's when 'n == 1' or 'n == 2'.

It is important to note that this solution while it is simple and direct, it is not efficient for large inputs of 'n' as it does redundant computations due to the overlapping subproblems in the recursion tree. This overlapping can lead us to compute the same Fibonacci number multiple times. This problem can be avoided by using techniques such as Dynamic Programming.

For instance, an illustration with 'fibonacci(5)', the recursion tree is as follows:

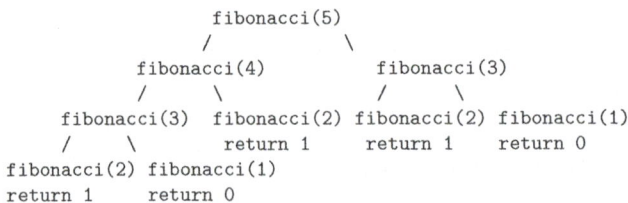

```
                fibonacci(5)
              /             \
        fibonacci(4)        fibonacci(3)
        /       \           /       \
  fibonacci(3) fibonacci(2) fibonacci(2) fibonacci(1)
    /     \      return 1    return 1    return 0
fibonacci(2) fibonacci(1)
return 1     return 0
```

As can be seen from the recursion tree, 'fibonacci(3)' and 'fibonacci(2)' are being calculated numerous times. With bigger values of 'n', the same computation increases exponentially, leading to inefficiency. This can be avoided with memoization or other Dynamic Programming techniques.

8.2 How would you solve the Tower of Hanoi problem using recursion?

The Tower of Hanoi problem is a mathematical puzzle. It consists of three poles and a number of disks of different sizes, which can slide onto any pole. The puzzle starts with the disks in a neat stack in ascending order of size on one rod, the smallest at the top, thus making a conical shape. The objective of the puzzle is to move the entire stack to another rod, obeying the following simple rules:

1. Only one disk can be moved at a time.

2. Each move consists of taking the upper disk from one of the stacks and placing it on top of another stack or on an empty rod.

3. No disk may be placed on top of a smaller disk.

We can solve the problem using a recursive approach. The key to the solution is to break the problem down into smaller subproblems.

We can write the recursive function to solve the problem as follows:

1. Move the top 'n−1' disks from pole 'A' (source pole) to pole 'B' (auxiliary pole), using pole 'C' (destination pole).

2. Move the remaining disk from pole 'A' to pole 'C'.

3. Move the 'n−1' disks from pole 'B' to pole 'C', using pole 'A'.

Let's denote this function as 'Hanoi(n, A, B, C)'. The pseudocode for the function is as follows:

```
function Hanoi(n, source, auxiliary, target) {
    if (n > 0) {
        // Move n-1 disks from source to auxiliary, using target as
            temporary pole
        Hanoi(n-1, source, target, auxiliary);

        // Move the nth disk from source to target
        print "Move␣disk␣" + n + "␣from␣pole␣" + source + "␣to␣pole␣"
            + target;

        // Move the n-1 disks that we left on auxiliary to target
        Hanoi(n-1, auxiliary, source, target);
    }
}
```

Then, to solve the problem with 'n' disks, you would call the function as 'Hanoi(n, 'A', 'B', 'C')'.

The time complexity of the algorithm is given by the recurrence relation 'T(n) = 2T(n-1) + O(1)'. First, we ignore the minor operations 'O(1)'. The solution to this recurrence relation results in $T(n) = 2^n - 1$ operations. Therefore, the time complexity of the Tower of Hanoi problem is $O(2^n)$.

This is because for each disk 'n', we execute a recursive function twice to solve the subproblem of size 'n-1'. Hence, we have '2T(n-1)'. The '+ O(1)' takes care of the moving operation.

The space complexity of the algorithm is 'O(n)'. This stems from the maximum depth of recursion we hit when using an explicit stack to keep track of function calls (recursion), which in the worst case is 'n' (where 'n' is the number of disks). Each function call requires a constant amount of space for housekeeping tasks and hence we get linear space complexity.

Let's solve the problem for 3 disks:

```
Step 1: Call `Hanoi(3, 'A', 'B', 'C')`

- Call `Hanoi(2, 'A', 'C', 'B')`

    - Call `Hanoi(1, 'A', 'B', 'C')`
        - Call `Hanoi(0, 'A', 'C', 'B')` - Base case, do nothing
        - Move disk 1 from pole A to pole C
        - Call `Hanoi(0, 'B', 'A', 'C')` - Base case, do nothing
    - Move disk 2 from pole A to pole B
    - Call `Hanoi(1, 'C', 'A', 'B')`
        - Call `Hanoi(0, 'C', 'B', 'A')` - Base case, do nothing
        - Move disk 1 from pole C to pole B
        - Call `Hanoi(0, 'A', 'C', 'B')` - Base case, do nothing

- Move disk 3 from pole A to pole C

- Call `Hanoi(2, 'B', 'A', 'C')`
    - Call `Hanoi(1, 'B', 'C', 'A')`
        - Call `Hanoi(0, 'B', 'A', 'C')` - Base case, do nothing
        - Move disk 1 from pole B to pole A
        - Call `Hanoi(0, 'C', 'B', 'A')` - Base case, do nothing
    - Move disk 2 from pole B to pole C
    - Call `Hanoi(1, 'A', 'B', 'C')`
        - Call `Hanoi(0, 'A', 'C', 'B')` - Base case, do nothing
        - Move disk 1 from pole A to pole C
        - Call `Hanoi(0, 'B', 'A', 'C')` - Base case, do nothing
```

This results in the sequence of moves:

- Move disk 1 from pole A to pole C

- Move disk 2 from pole A to pole B

- Move disk 1 from pole C to pole B

- Move disk 3 from pole A to pole C

- Move disk 1 from pole B to pole A

- Move disk 2 from pole B to pole C

- Move disk 1 from pole A to pole C

So, this is the list of moves to solve the Tower of Hanoi problem for 3 disks.

8.3 How would you implement the coin change problem using dynamic programming?

The coin change problem is a problem of finding the number of ways of making changes for a particular amount of money using coins of given denominations.

We can solve this problem using dynamic programming by creating a solution array to keep track of the solutions for the problems. Let's assume that our given coin denominations are d[0], d[1], ..., d[m-1].

Let's define an array dp[], where dp[i] will be storing the number of solutions for value i. We need m+1 rows as in the bottom-up approach, dp[i] will be computed using the solution to previous i values.

Here is the iterative approach using dynamic programming:

Define dp[N+1] where N is the amount you are making change for. dp[i] will be storing the number of solutions for value i.

Algorithm pseudo code:

```
def coinChange(coins, amount):
    # Initialize dp array
    dp = [0]*(amount+1)

    # Base case: There is exactly 1 way to create a sum of 0, that
        is using no coin
    dp[0] = 1

    # Iterate over all coins
    for i in range(0, len(coins)):
        # Compute the number of ways for all values
        # greater than the coin value
        for j in range(coins[i], amount+1):
            dp[j] += dp[j - coins[i]]
```

```
# Return the number of ways to make the amount using coins
return dp[amount]
```

This dynamic programming solution has O(mN) time complexity as each subproblem takes O(1) time to solve, where m is the array length and N is the amount.

You can visualize this process in a matrix as follows:

dp	0	1	2	3	4	5	6	7	8	9	10
1	1	1	1	1	1	1	1	1	1	1	1
2	1	1	2	2	3	3	4	4	5	5	6
5	1	1	2	2	3	4	5	6	7	8	10

For example, the number of ways to make change for 10 using coin denominations [1, 2, 5] is 10.

8.4 Can you solve the knapsack problem using dynamic programming?

The knapsack problem can be solved using Dynamic Programming. The knapsack problem is a problem in combinatorial optimization. Given a set of items, each with a weight and a value, determine the number of each item to include in a collection so that the total weight is less than or equal to a given limit and the total value is as large as possible.

Let's say you are given a set of 'n' items, each item 'i' has some weight 'w[i]' and a value 'v[i]'. You are also given a maximum weight 'W'. The goal is to choose items with maximum total value such that their total weight is not more than 'W'.

We can define a 2D table 'dp[i][j]' where 'i' ranges from 0 to 'n' (the item index) and 'j' ranges from 0 to 'W' (the maximum weight). Each cell 'dp[i][j]' represents the maximum value we can get by considering the first 'i' items and a maximum weight of 'j'.

The base case for this problem is 'dp[i][0]' and 'dp[0][j]', which represent the cases where the maximum weight is 0 (we can't choose any items) and where we don't consider any items, respectively. In both cases, the maximum value is 0.

Then, for filling in the rest of the table, we follow this recursive relation:

```
if w[i] > j :
    dp[i][j] = dp[i-1][j]
else:
    dp[i][j] = max(dp[i-1][j], v[i] + dp[i-1][j-w[i]])
```

Explicitly, this recursive relation means that, if the weight of the current item is more than the current maximum weight, we can't include this item, so the maximum value is the same as the maximum value not considering this item. Otherwise, the maximum value is either the maximum value not considering this item, or the value of this item plus the maximum value we can get considering the remaining weight.

Finally, 'dp[n][W]' will give the maximum total value including the first 'n' items for a maximum weight 'W'.

The pseudo code for the DP approach:

```
function knapSack(W, w, v, n):
  K = array of [n+1][W+1]

  // Build table K[][] in bottom up manner
  for i from 0 to n:
    for w from 0 to W:
      if i==0 or w==0:
```

```
        K[i][w] = 0
    else if w[i-1] <= w:
        K[i][w] = max(v[i-1] + K[i-1][w-w[i-1]], K[i-1][w])
    else:
        K[i][w] = K[i-1][w]

return K[n][W] // this will return the maximum value that can be
    put in the knapsack of capacity W
```

This dynamic programming solution for the knapsack problem
has a time complexity of 'O(nW)' and a space complexity of
'O(nW)', where 'n' is the number of items and 'W' is the maximum weight. This is because it fills up a 2D table of size 'nW'
with the maximum values for each subproblem.

8.5   Can you write a recursive function to generate all permutations of a string?

Generating permutations of a string is a classical problem that
employs the method of recursion in a crucial way. Here is a
simple Python function that generates all the permutations of
a string:

```
def permutations(string, step = 0):

    # if we've reached the end, print the permutation
    if step == len(string):
        print("".join(string))

    # everything to the right of step has not been swapped yet
    for i in range(step, len(string)):

        # copy the string (store as list)
        string_copy = [c for c in string]

        # swap the current index with the step
        string_copy[step], string_copy[i] = string_copy[i], 
        string_copy[step]

        # recurse on the portion of the string that has not been 
        swapped yet (now it's index will begin with step + 1)
        permutations(string_copy, step + 1)
```

Explanation for this Python function:

1. If we're at the end of the string, we print the permutation.

2. We iterate from our progress in the function so far to the end of the string. Currently, our progress is denoted by 'step'.

3. We copy the string and swap the current character with the character at the position of our current progress.

4. We recursively call the function on this copy with the progress incremented.

Consider an example:

```
permutations("ABC")
```

It will generate the output:

```
ABC
ACB
BAC
BCA
CBA
CAB
```

Note: The recursion tree follows the Depth-First Search (DFS) approach, thus generating all possible permutations. Each level of recursion considers swapping a fixed character of the string with all the other characters that follows it. Consequently, the recursion explores all options for each position (from left to right) in the string and generates all the permutations.

8.6 How would you solve the problem of climbing stairs (you can climb 1 or 2 steps at a time) using dynamic programming?

This is a classic problem that can be solved using dynamic programming. The problem can be formulated as follows:

You are climbing a stair that has 'n' steps. At each step, you can either climb 1 or 2 steps. In how many distinct ways can you climb to the top?

To approach this problem from a dynamic programming perspective, let's denote 'dp[i]' as the number of distinct ways to reach the 'i-th' step. We want to compute the value 'dp[n]', which will give us the total number of distinct ways to reach the top with 'n' steps.

The base cases for this problem are when 'n = 1' and 'n = 2'. If there is only one step, there is only one way to climb it: climbing one step. Similarly, if there are two steps, there are two ways to climb them: climbing two steps at once or climbing one step twice. So, we have:

```
dp[1] = 1
dp[2] = 2
```

For 'n > 2', the number of distinct ways to reach step 'n' can be computed from 'dp[n-1]' and 'dp[n-2]'. This is because, from the '(n-1)-th' step, we can take one step to reach the 'n-th' step, and from the '(n-2)-th' step, we can take two steps to reach the 'n-th' step. This gives us:

```
dp[n] = dp[n-1] + dp[n-2]
```

With these equations, we can start filling up our 'dp' array from 'dp[1]' up to 'dp[n]'. Here's a simple Python example:

```
def climbStairs(n):
    if n <= 2:
        return n
    dp = [0 for _ in range(n+1)]
    dp[1] = 1
    dp[2] = 2
    for i in range(3, n+1):
        dp[i] = dp[i-1] + dp[i-2]
    return dp[-1]
```

Using dynamic programming in this way, we achieve a time complexity of 'O(n)' and a space complexity of 'O(n)'. However, since 'dp[i]' only depends on 'dp[i-1]' and 'dp[i-2]', we can reduce the space complexity to 'O(1)' by only keeping the last two calculated values:

```
def climbStairs(n):
    if n <= 2:
        return n
    a, b = 1, 2
    for _ in range(3, n+1):
        a, b = b, a+b
    return b
```

This solution maintains a similar time complexity 'O(n)' but reduces the space complexity to 'O(1)'.

8.7 Can you find the longest common subsequence of two strings using dynamic programming?

The Longest Common Subsequence (LCS) problem is a classic computer science problem often solved using dynamic programming. Given two sequences, this problem involves finding the longest subsequence present in both of them. A subsequence is a sequence that can be derived from another sequence by deleting some or no elements without changing the order of the remaining elements.

Here's how you can find the longest common subsequence of two strings using dynamic programming:

Let's denote the two input strings as 'X[0..m-1]' and 'Y[0..n-1]'. For this process, we can start by initially defining a 2D matrix 'dp[][]' of size '(m+1)x(n+1)'.

Here, 'dp[i][j]' will hold the length of the longest common subsequence of the prefixes 'X[0..i-1]' and 'Y[0..j-1]'.

To clarify, here is the formula that will be used:

$$dp[i][j] = \begin{cases} 0 & \text{if } i = 0 \text{ or } j = 0 \\ dp[i-1][j-1] + 1 & \text{if } X[i-1] = Y[j-1] \\ \max(dp[i-1][j], dp[i][j-1]) & \text{if } X[i-1] \neq Y[j-1] \end{cases}$$

The approach behind this algorithm is as follows:

1. If 'X[i-1]' is equal to 'Y[j-1]', this means we have found a matching character in both strings. Thus, the LCS up to 'i,j' is the LCS up to 'i-1,j-1' extended by this matching character, hence we add 1 to 'dp[i-1][j-1]'.

2. If 'X[i-1]' is not equal to 'Y[j-1]', we have a choice to ignore either 'X[i-1]' or 'Y[j-1]'. Select the previous cell that has the maximum LCS, i.e., maximum of 'dp[i][j-1]' or 'dp[i-1][j]'.

The LCS of the complete strings 'X' and 'Y' is given by 'dp[m][n]' which is the last cell.

For example, let 'X = "ABCBDAB"' and 'Y = "BDCAB"'. The

LCS is '"BCAB"'. Following the above approach, here is what the filled table would look like:

```
    "" B D C A B
""  0  0 0 0 0 0
A   0  0 0 0 1 1
B   0  1 1 1 1 2
C   0  1 1 2 2 2
B   0  1 1 2 2 3
D   0  1 2 2 2 3
A   0  1 2 2 3 3
B   0  1 2 2 3 4
```

Every cell 'dp[i][j]' holds the LCS length of the prefixes 'X[0...i-1]' and 'Y[0...j-1]', thus the LCS length for whole 'X' and 'Y' is 'dp[m][n] = 4', which matches with our LCS string '"BCAB"' length. So, the bottom-right cell has the length of the LCS.

Bear in mind, this algorithm does not return the actual LCS, but only its length. To find the actual LCS string, one has to backtrack from the 'dp[m][n]' cell according to the following rules: - If 'X[i-1] = Y[j-1]', it means that this character is part of the LCS string, so add 'X[i-1]' (or 'Y[j-1]') to the LCS string and go diagonally up to 'dp[i-1][j-1]'. - If 'X[i-1] != Y[j-1]', then go to the cell that contains the maximum value, which can be either 'dp[i-1][j]' or 'dp[i][j-1]'. If both have the same value, either choice can work.

This backtrack approach will complete the LCS algorithm for finding not just the length, but also the LCS string.

Time complexity of this solution is 'O(m*n)' (where m and n are string lengths) for the LCS length computing and 'O(m+n)' for the LCS string recovering, so overall linear in terms of strings length.

8.8 Can you find the number of ways to decode a message given a coding scheme using dynamic programming?

Let's assume that we have "A" assigned as 1, "B" as 2, ..., "Z" as 26. So given a digit-encoded message, such as "123", that could be decoded in several ways: "ABC" (1 2 3), "LC" (12 3), or "AW" (1 23). So the message "123" has 3 ways of being decoded. Let's use dynamic programming to solve this problem.

To get started, we need to build an array dp[] of size n + 1 to store the decoding count. The count dp[i] will be the count of decoding for the sequence from index 1 to i.

First, we initialize dp[0] = 1 since there's only one way to decode a sequence of length 0, and dp[1] = 1, because there's only one way to decode a sequence of length 1.

From here, we start a for loop from 2 to n (length of the digit), and for each index i, we check two things:

(a) If the last digit is not 0, then there could be ways associated with the last digit, we increment count dp[i] = dp[i-1] (b) If second last or last two digits form a number less than or equal to 26, then we increment dp[i] += dp[i-2]

So the pseudo code will look like:

```
def count_decoding(digits, n):
    dp = [0] * (n+1)
    dp[0] = 1
    dp[1] = 1

    for i in range(2, n+1):
        if digits[i-1] > '0':
```

```
        dp[i] = dp[i-1]
    if (digits[i-2] == '1' or (digits[i-2] == '2' and digits[i-1]
        < '7')):
        dp[i] += dp[i-2]
return dp[n]
```

With this, you can calculate the number of ways a sequence can be decoded.

For instance, let's take "1234" as an example:

1. i = 2, "1234" -> last digit is '2' and 12 is between 1 to 26, so dp[2] = dp[1] + dp[0] = 2

2. i = 3, "1234" -> last digit is '3' and 23 is between 1 to 26, so dp[3] = dp[2] + dp[1] = 3

3. i = 4, "1234" -> last digit is '4' but 34 is not between 1 to 26, so dp[4] = dp[3] = 3.

So there are 3 ways to decode the message "1234".

Finally, dp[n] returns the total number of ways the given sequence can be decoded.

8.9 How would you solve the problem of unique paths in a grid using dynamic programming?

The problem of "unique paths in a grid" can be described as follows. We have an m x n grid, and we are situated at the top-left corner which is at coordinate (0, 0). We need to reach the bottom-right corner at coordinate (m-1, n-1). We are allowed to only move right or down. The problem is to calculate the total number of unique paths possible to reach the destination from the starting position.

This problem can be solved using dynamic programming (DP). In dynamic programming, we divide the problem into smaller subproblems, and we store the results of these subproblems. If we again encounter the same subproblem, we don't have to solve it again; we can directly use the stored result.

Here's how we can implement a solution using dynamic programming:

- We initialize a 2D array dp of size (m x n). Elements of dp represent the number of unique paths to that particular coordinate (i,j).

- We initialize the first row and the first column as 1, because there is only one way to reach any cell in the first row or first column i.e., by moving right or down only.

- Then we move towards the remaining cells (except the cells in the first row and first column). The number of ways to reach to a cell (i, j) would be the sum of number of ways to reach the cell (i, j-1) and the cell (i-1, j).

Here is how it can be expressed in code:

```
def uniquePaths(m, n):
    dp = [[1]*n for _ in range(m)]

    for i in range(1, m):
        for j in range(1, n):
            dp[i][j] = dp[i-1][j] + dp[i][j-1]

    return dp[m-1][n-1]
```

Let's take m=3 and n=7 for instance, the 2D dp array would look like this:

```
1  1  1   1   1   1   1
1  2  3   4   5   6   7
1  3  6  10  15  21  28
```

Time complexity of this solution is O(m*n) and space complexity is also O(m*n) as we are using an extra 2D DP table.

The last element dp[m-1][n-1] gives you the total unique paths from (0,0) to (m-1, n-1). In this case, that is 28 paths.

8.10 Can you implement a function to compute the nth number in the Fibonacci sequence using dynamic programming?

Computing the nth Fibonacci number using dynamic programming is pretty straightforward, you just need to store each Fibonacci number as you compute it and use previously computed numbers to compute the next ones.

Here is a simple Python implementation:

```
def fib(n):
    F = [0, 1] + [0]*(n-1)
    for i in range(2, n+1):
        F[i] = F[i-1] + F[i-2]
    return F[n]
```

This function creates an empty list 'F' of size 'n+1' and initializes 'F[0]' and 'F[1]' to '0' and '1' respectively. After that, it computes each 'F[i]' as 'F[i-1] + F[i-2]' for 'i = 2' to 'n'.

This approach allows it to calculate the nth Fibonacci number in $O(n)$ time, which is much better than the naive recursive solution that takes $O(2^n)$ time.

We can also optimize this function by only keeping the last two previously computed Fibonacci numbers:

```
def fib(n):
    a, b = 0, 1
    for _ in range(n):
        a, b = b, a+b
    return a
```

This version of the function computes the nth Fibonacci number in $O(n)$ time and $O(1)$ space.

If you're interested in mathematical representations, here's a brief overview:

The Fibonacci sequence is formally defined by the recurrence relation:

'F(n) = F(n-1) + F(n-2)'

with 'F(0) = 0' and 'F(1) = 1'. Hence, the formula used in the dynamic programming-based implementations is 'F[i] = F[i-1] + F[i-2]' for 'i = 2' to 'n'.

Chapter 9

Bit Manipulation Problems

9.1 How would you check if a number is a power of 2 using bit manipulation?

If a number is a power of 2, it has one set bit in its binary representation and all other bits are unset.

Here is the binary representation of powers of 2:

$$2^0 = 1 \qquad\qquad = 0001_b$$
$$2^1 = 2 \qquad\qquad = 0010_b$$
$$2^2 = 4 \qquad\qquad = 0100_b$$
$$2^3 = 8 \qquad\qquad = 1000_b$$

As you can see, these binary representations only have one bit set (one '1') and the rest are zeroes. This is a defining characteristic of powers of 2.

We can express this characteristic using bit manipulation. If 'n' is a power of 2, then 'n' AND 'n-1' will be '0'.

Let's examine this. If 'n' is a power of 2, we have a binary representation like '1000...0'. Now, 'n-1' will be '0111...1'. When we do a bitwise AND operation ('&'), every bit of the result will be '0' because '1' AND '0' yields '0' and '0' AND '1' also yields '0'.

More formally, let's represent the number as 2^k. Then the binary representation of 2^k in a sufficiently large number of bits is:

$$2^k = 1000...0$$

And $2^k - 1$ is:

$$2^k - 1 = 0111...1$$

So, the bitwise AND of these two numbers:

$$2^k \& (2^k - 1) = 0000...0 = 0$$

You can implement this as a function in any language that supports bitwise operations. For example, in Java:

```
boolean isPowerOfTwo(int n) {
  if(n <= 0) return false;
  return (n & (n - 1)) == 0;
}
```

This function first checks if the number is positive (since the method doesn't work for negatives or zero), then it returns whether 'n & (n - 1) == 0'. If 'n' is power of 2, this will be 'true', otherwise 'false'.

9.2 Can you write a function to count the number of bits that are set to 1 in a given number?

You could implement this using bitwise operations in many programming languages. Here is an example of how to implement this in Python:

```
def count_set_bits(n):
    count = 0
    while n:
        n &= n - 1
        count += 1
    return count
```

You would call the function count_set_bits with the number for which you want to count the number of set bits. For example, if you want to count the number of set bits in the binary representation of the number 5 (which is 101 in binary), you would call:

```
print(count_set_bits(5)) # Output: 2
```

Explanation: The code keeps resetting the rightmost set bit of the number until there are no set bits left, and it counts the number of operations this takes. This is done through the line 'n &= n - 1', which in each iteration, resets the rightmost set bit of n (subtracting 1 flips the rightmost set bit of n and all bits to the right of it, and taking bitwise-AND with n resets these flipped bits).

The time complexity of the function depends on the number of set bits in the number. If the number of set bits is b, then the runtime is $O(b)$, because each operation removes a set bit.

For example, consider the 8-bit integer 01100100. Here's how the operations proceed:

$$n = 01100100$$
$$n - 1 = 01100011$$
$$\underline{n \& (n - 1) = 01100000}$$
$$n = 01100000$$
$$n - 1 = 01011111$$
$$\underline{n \& (n - 1) = 01000000}$$
$$n = 01000000$$
$$n - 1 = 00111111$$
$$n \& (n - 1) = 00000000$$

We have to repeat the procedure three times (which is the number of set bits in the original number), so the complexity is indeed O(b).

9.3 How would you swap the values of two integers without using any additional variables?

Swapping the values of two integers without using any additional variables can be achieved using mathematical operations. Here's how you do it.

Let's say you are given two integers 'a' and 'b'.

The first step is to store the sum of 'a' and 'b' in 'a'. This makes 'a' carry both the information of 'a' and 'b'.

$$a = a + b$$

Now, 'a' is equivalent to 'a+b'. To get 'b' from 'a', subtract the original 'b' from 'a':

$$b = a - b$$

Given that 'a' was 'a+b', 'b' now becomes 'a'.

Finally, to get 'a', subtract the new 'b' (previously 'a') from 'a':

$$a = a - b$$

This series of operations effectively swaps 'a' and 'b' without using any temporary variables.

Here's a sample code that demonstrates this procedure:

```
def swap(a,b):
    a = a+b
    b = a-b
    a = a-b
    return a,b

print(swap(3,4))
```

This code swaps 'a' and 'b' in place without creating additional variables. Please note that this is really more of a programming puzzle solution and may not be the best solution when taking considerations of performance, potential Overflow risk and readability in real-world cases.

9.4 Can you find the only non-repeating number in an array where every element repeats twice except one, using bit manipulation?

We can find the non-repeating number in an array where every other element repeats twice using bit manipulation. This can be achieved using the XOR bitwise operator.

The XOR operation ("exclusive or") is a binary operation that takes two bits and returns 1 if exactly one of the bits is 1. In other words, it returns true if the two bits are opposite.

The XOR operation has two properties which are very useful in this context:

1) 'A XOR A = 0'

2) 'A XOR 0 = A'

3) 'A XOR B XOR A = B'

If we XOR all elements in the array, all the elements which are repeated twice will become 0 (because 'A XOR A = 0'), and we are left with the element which is only present once as the result.

Suppose we have an array 'arr[] = 2, 3, 5, 4, 5, 3, 4'.

If we XOR all the numbers together:

'(2 3 5 4 5 3 4)'

We can reorder as:

'((2 2) (3 3) (4 4) (5 5)) 5'

Each pair of the same number will XOR to 0, leaving us with:

'0 5'

Remember 'A XOR 0 = A', therefore we get '5' which is the number that has no duplicate in the array.

A Python example code:

```
def find_single(nums):
    res = 0
    for num in nums:
        res ^= num
    return res
```

For an array 'arr[] = 2, 3, 5, 4, 5, 3, 4', calling 'find_single(arr)' would return '5'.

9.5 How would you reverse the bits of a given binary number?

To reverse the bits of a given binary number, we can iterate through the bits of the number from the right side, shifting the bits of the reversed number, and pushing the bit from the original number onto the reversed number. Here's a step-by-step algorithm:

1. Set 'reversed_number' to 0 (where we will collect the reversed bits)

2. While 'number' is not 0, iterate:

   1. Bitwise shift right 'number' by 1 and set to 'number'. In code: 'number » 1'.

   2. Bitwise shift left 'reversed_number' by 1 and set to 'reversed_number'. In code: 'reversed_number « 1'.

   3. Get the least significant bit from 'number' (bit at the rightmost side), let's call it 'bit'. In code: 'bit = number & 1'.

   4. Bitwise OR 'reversed_number' with 'bit', and set to 'reversed_number'. In code: 'reversed_number = reversed_number | bit'.

In Python, the explained algorithm would look like this:

```
def reverse_bits(number):
    reversed_number = 0
    while number != 0:
        number = number >> 1
        reversed_number = reversed_number << 1
        bit = number & 1
        reversed_number = reversed_number | bit
    return reversed_number
```

Let's take an example where the input binary number is 12 (in binary 1100):

1. Initially, reversed_number=0 (in binary 0).

2. In the first iteration, we right shift number by 1, making it 6 (110).

3. Now we left shift the reversed_number by 1, it remains 0.

4. Extract the last bit of number, which is 0.

5. OR operation between reversed_number (0) and bit (0) remains 0.

6. In the next iteration, number becomes 3 (11), and reversed_number is still 0.

7. Bit extraction from number gives us 1 this time.

8. OR operation between reversed_number (0) and bit (1) gives us 1.

9. After a few more iterations, the original number becomes 0, and the reversed_number becomes 3 (in binary 0011), which is the reverse of initial binary 1100.

An important note: this algorithm assumes that the inputs and outputs fit in a designated number of bits (like 32 bits for int in Python). If you could potentially have large integers that are over 32 bits, you'd need to modify the algorithm to accommodate that.

9.6 Can you find the two non-repeating numbers in an array where every element repeats twice except two, using bit manipulation?

You can find two non-repeating numbers in an array where every other element repeats twice except two. This can be achieved through bit manipulation, one of the key ideas behind the XOR operation. Here is how you can do it step by step.

1. Take XOR of all the elements in the array. XOR of all elements in array will give XOR of the two non-repeating elements, which we'll call xXory. Since we are XORing same numbers twice, they will cancel out each other, and non repeating numbers XOR will remain.

For instance, consider the array: 2, 4, 7, 9, 2, 4. The XOR of all elements yields '79'.

2. Take any set bit (bit that is 1) of xXory and divide the elements of array into two groups. One group which has the same bit set and another group which has this bit unset. We can take any set bit, let's say kth bit from right. One non-repeating number will belong to the first group and the other non-repeating number will be in the second group. By performing XOR operation on the two groups individually, we get the two numbers.

For example, let's say 1st bit from right of '79' is set. Divide array into two groups and do XOR on elements. Group1: 2, 7, 2 => '272' gives 7 which is one of the non-repeating number. Group2: 4, 9, 4 => '494' gives 9 which is the other non-repeat number.

Here's the Python code snippet for better understanding:

```
def findTwoNonRepeatingNumbers(arr):
    xor = arr[0]
    for i in range(1, len(arr)):
        xor ^= arr[i]

    setBitNo = xor & ~(xor-1)

    x, y = 0, 0
    for i in range(len(arr)):
```

```
        if((arr[i] & setBitNo) != 0):
            x = x ^ arr[i]
        else:
            y = y ^ arr[i]

    return x, y
arr = [2, 3, 7, 9, 11, 2, 3, 11]
print(findTwoNonRepeatingNumbers(arr))
```

This code first takes XOR of all elements, gets the last set bit of 'xor' and separates these two non-repeating numbers(x, y) into two groups based on last set bit. Performing XOR on these two groups separately gives these two numbers.

The complexity of this solution is O(n), which is the best we can achieve for this problem.

Please note this method only works when there are exactly two non-repeating elements. Other cases require different handling.

9.7 Can you find the maximum of two integers without using if-else or any other comparison operator?

it is possible to determine the maximum of two integers without using if-else or any other comparison operator. This can be done using bitwise operators and principles of arithmetic in the world of computer science.

Let's denote the two numbers as 'a' and 'b'.

The key idea is to get the difference between 'b' and 'a', and then extract the sign of this difference, which can either be 0 when 'b >= a' or 1 when 'b < a'.

Firstly, notice that we can obtain the sign of any number 'x' by performing the bitwise AND operation on 'x' and the most significant bit mask, and then shifting right by 31 bits (on a 32-bit system). This gives us 1 if 'x' is negative and 0 if 'x' is non-negative.

Therefore, the expression for the sign of the difference 'b - a' is:

```
diff = b - a
sign = (diff & (1 << 31)) >> 31
```

So, now we have the sign of the difference, we can use it to return either 'a' or 'b' as the maximum.

We can create an expression that equals 'a' when 'sign = 0' and 'b' when 'sign = 1', which is equivalent to:

```
maximum = a * (sign ^ 1) + b * sign
```

Here is a python code snippet which demonstrates this:

```
def maxOfTwo(a, b):
    diff = b - a
    sign = (diff & (1 << 31)) >> 31 # get the sign of diff
    maximum = a * (sign ^ 1) + b * sign
    return maximum
```

This solution works because the bitwise XOR of any bit with 1 flips the bit, whereas XOR with 0 leaves it unchanged.

Keep in mind that this solution may not work as expected with overflow integers and corner cases should be handled properly in a production-level code.

Moreover, it's worth noting that this solution assumes the numbers are 32 bits wide, but it can be easily generalized to work for numbers of any bit width.

9.8 How would you add two numbers without using arithmetic operators?

You can add two numbers without using arithmetic operators by using bitwise operators. This is mainly a binary level manipulation. Bitwise operators include AND (&), OR(|), XOR(), Left Shift(«), and Right Shift(») operators. To perform addition without an arithmetic operator, half adder logic is used, which is a basic single bit adder designed using XOR and AND gates. The XOR gate works as the ADDER while the AND gate works as Binary Carry calculator.

Below is the method in Python for adding two numbers without using arithmetic operators:

```python
def add(a, b):
    # Iterate till there is no carry
    while (b != 0):
        # carry now contains common set bits of a and b
        carry = a & b

        # Sum of bits of a and b where at least one of the bits is
            not set
        a = a ^ b

        # Carry is shifted by one so that adding it to a gives the
            required sum
        b = carry << 1

    return a

# Test this function
print(add(20, 30))
```

In this code:

1. The expression 'carry = a & b' produces a binary number that has '1's where 'a' and 'b' both have 1's. That's why it's called carry - these '1's should be carried over and added to the next power of two.

2. The expression 'a = a ᵇ' produces a binary number that has '1's

where 'a' and 'b' have '1's exclusively - when 'a' has '1' and 'b' has
'0', and vice versa. So, this step provides a partial sum.

3. The carry is then shifted one bit to the left '(carry « 1)' and
added to the partial sum in the first step.

4. The while loop continues until there is no carry, which means
that all '1's that should be carried over and added have been added.

Note that the code example given is in Python, however one
can use the same logic to write this function in many other
languages. The code might not work with languages in which
bitwise operations do not work well on the signed numbers.
Bitwise operation works perfectly fine with unsigned numbers
in C/C++. It's important that you confirm whether bitwise
operation works as expected for signed numbers in all cases
your programming language.

Let's understand this using an example:

If we want to add 2(0010) and 3(0011),

Step 1. Carry = a & b = (0010) & (0011) = 2 (0010)

Step 2: a = a ᵬ = 23 = 1 (0001)

Step 3: b = carry « 1 = 2 « 1 = 2*2 = 4 (0100)

Then, repeat these steps:

Step 1: Carry = a & b = 1 & 4 = 0 (0000)

Step 2: a = a ᵬ = 14 = 5 (0101)

Step 3: b = carry « 1 = 0 « 1 = 0 (0000)

Now, 'b' becomes '0' so we end the loop and return 'a' as the sum, which is indeed 5.

9.9 How would you determine the number of bits required to convert one given integer into another?

To find the number of bits required to convert one integer into another, you can use the XOR bitwise operator. The XOR operator returns a bit where the corresponding bits of two operands are different. This means, if the corresponding bit values of two integers are different on the XOR operation, we would need to change that bit in the conversion.

Here's your algorithm:

1. Compute the XOR of two numbers.

2. Count the number of set bits in the result from step 1. This will be the number of bits we need to change.

Code Example in Python

You can use this Python code as an example to compute the number of bits required to convert one integer into another.

```python
def countBitsToConvert(a: int, b: int) -> int:
    # Step 1: Compute the XOR of two numbers
    n = a ^ b

    # Step 2: Count the number of set bits in the result
    count = 0
    while n:
        count += n & 1
        n >>= 1
    return count

# Test the function
a = 14 # represented as 01110 in binary
b = 31 # represented as 11111 in binary
```

```
print(countBitsToConvert(a, b)) # output: 1
```

In this example, the binary representation of numbers 14 and 31 is 01110 and 11111 respectively. Their XOR operation gives 10001. There is only one bit set (the bit in position 4 counting from zero from right to left), hence the number of bits required to convert 14 to 31 is 1.

The time complexity of the above algorithm is $O(log\ n)$, and the space complexity is $O(1)$.

You can also use the built-in Python method 'bin()' to calculate the number of set bits in a simple way, like so:

```
def countBitsToConvert(a: int, b: int) -> int:
    return bin(a^b).count('1')
```

This method first calculates 'a XOR b' and returns a binary string. Then the 'count('1')' method counts the number of '1's in the binary string, which is equal to the number of bits required to convert 'a' to 'b'. The time complexity is still $O(log\ n)$ and the space complexity is $O(1)$.

9.10   Can you find the rightmost set bit in a binary number?

It is possible to find the rightmost set bit (i.e., 1) in a binary number using bitwise operations in programming.

Firstly, let's understand the bitwise AND (&) operation. The operation takes two numbers as operands and does AND on every bit of the binary representations of the numbers. If both bits in the compared position are 1, the bit in the resulting binary representation is 1 (1 & 1 = 1). Otherwise, the result is 0 (0 & 0 = 0, 0 & 1 = 0, 1 & 0 = 0).

To find the rightmost set bit, we can take advantage of this operation and the properties of binary number subtraction. When a binary number (let's call it n) is subtracted by 1, the rightmost 1 in the binary representation of n flips to 0, and all the bits to the right of this bit also flip.

For example,

```
Let n = 40, which is 101000 in binary
n-1 = 39, which is 100111 in binary
```

When you perform bitwise AND operation on n and n - 1, only the part up to the rightmost set bit in n (including this bit) becomes 0.

```
n&(n-1) = 101000 & 100111 = 100000, which is 32 in decimal
```

To reveal the rightmost bit, we can subtract the result from the original number:

```
n-(n&(n-1)) = 101000 - 100000 = 1000 = 8 in decimal
```

This gives the rightmost set bit in the binary representation of n which is the number 8 in decimal.

So the formula to find the rightmost set bit can be given by:

```
r = n - (n & (n - 1))
```

Where 'n' represents the binary number and 'r' is the rightmost set bit. Here, '&' refers the bitwise AND operation.

For instance, if you want to find the rightmost set bit of 40(101000 in binary), you would do:

```
40 - (40 & (40 - 1)) = 8
```

This formula indicates that the rightmost set bit of the binary representation of 40 is 8 (which is 23, corresponding to the fourth bit from right in binary representation).

Chapter 10

Understanding System Design

10.1 Can you describe how you would design a URL shortening service like Bitly?

Designing a URL shortening service like Bitly involves several considerations including redirecting to long URLs, generating short URLs, and scaling the system.

1. **Redirecting to long URLs**: The core functionality of a URL shortening service is to take a short URL and redirect the user to the long URL.

2. **Generating Short URLs**: The another main functionality is to generate unique short URLs for any provided long

URL.

3. **Scaling the System**: It's crucial to anticipate that the service needs to handle a large number of read/write requests.

Here is a high-level breakdown of how you could design such a system:

A. **Hashing**: An immediate approach that might come to mind is to use a hash function. Hash the full URL and keep it in the database. This will involve the use of an MD5 or SHA256 like hash function.

$$H = \text{Hash}(URL)$$

The problem here is that the hash functions will generate a fixed length (for example, 256 bits for SHA256) hash, which might be too long for a URL shortening service. Therefore, you need to take a subset of the output hash, which makes collision possible. However, you can handle collision by:

- Using a different hash function
- Having the user choose another URL
- Appending sequence numbers

B. **Generating Unique Keys**: Another approach would be to generate an incrementing sequence of numbers and convert them to a base62 (characters a-z, A-Z, 0-9) string.

Here's how you can generate a unique key:

URL_id = Decimal_to_base62(auto-increment-ID)

And for redirection, get the URL_id back:

URL = base62_to_decimal(URL_id)

C. **System Design Considerations**:

- **Database and Storage**: You should select a storage meeting your requirements regarding data durability, data consistency, low latency etc. Considering the case of a URL shortening service, NoSQL databases like Cassandra or key-value stores may be a good fit.

- **Load Balancer and Cache**: Implementing a Load Balancer could distribute the network load evenly to the webservers, making the application more reliable. Also, a cache like Redis can store popular URLs in memory to reduce latency.

- **Distributed Systems and Sharding**: In order to achieve scalability and handle more URLs, you may consider using distributed systems and partition the data using sharding techniques.

D. **Designing the URL shortening service for Hight Availability**: A URL shortening service should be highly available. This demands strong consistency between multiple DB instances. Each write operation would undertake more time as it needs to be updated globally. The eventual consistency model works better here. Databases like DynamoDB offer tunable consistency.

Here is a basic diagram how everything might interact:

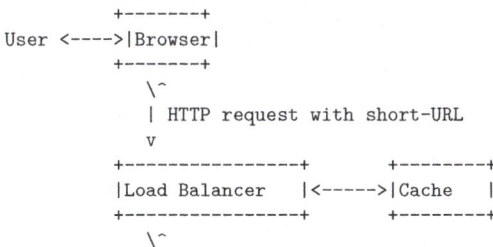

```
          +--------+
User <---->|Browser|
          +--------+
            \^
            | HTTP request with short-URL
            v
        +----------------+         +--------+
        |Load Balancer   |<----->|Cache   |
        +----------------+         +--------+
            \^
```

```
| Distributed to Web servers
   v
+----------------+
|Web server      |<----->|Database|
+----------------+
```

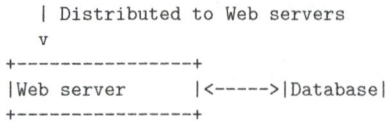

Please note that all the above are high-level ideas on how to design a URL shortening service and doesn't cover the detailed implementation.

10.2 How would you design a global File Storage Service like Google Drive?

Designing a global File Storage Service like Google Drive involves several factors. Let's consider the business requirements and system requirements separately.

1. Business Requirements:

- Massive storage: A system needs to store billions of files.

- Fast access: The system needs to be able to quickly store and retrieve these files.

- Sharing: The system needs the ability to share files and folders, giving either read-only or read/write access to specific users.

- Realtime synchronization: The system should mirror any changes made to the file over all the devices of the user.

- Data consistency: All replicas of the files should offer the same view of the data.

2. System Requirements:

- Horizontally scalable: The system should be capable of scaling as the amount of data increases.

- High availability: All files should be available for access at any point in time.

- Data durability: The system should be robust against data loss.

- Security and privacy: The data should be securely stored, with sensitive data being encrypted.

3. Key Design Considerations

To build such a File Storage Service, we need to consider the following:

- File Metadata management
- File data and its version management
- File sharing and collaboration
- Resilient against failures

Here is a high-level breakdown of the system design:

1. File Metadata Management:

To store metadata of all files, Google Drive possibly uses Bigtable, a distributed storage system for managing structured data. Each file could be represented by an object containing:

FileID : Unique identifier of the file

FileName : Name of the file

CreatedTime : Creation timestamp

UpdatedTime : Timestamp of the last update

Owner : User who uploaded the file

Size : Size of the file

ShareInfo : Info about the users file is shared with

Location : Location of the file in the user's directory structure

We can use consistent hashing for distribution of files among servers.

2. File Data and Its Version Management:

Google Drive uses another distributed storage system, Google Cloud Storage, to store the actual file data. Each file is divided into several chunks, and each chunk is replicated over multiple data stores for durability and availability.

Whenever a file gets updated, the changed chunks are versioned and stored as a new copy (like Copy-on-Write), while the old versions are still kept for some time.

3. File Sharing and Collaboration:

For file sharing, we need to store the sharing list, which contains users/groups the file shared with and their access level (read/write).

When multiple users edit the same file, to avoid write-write conflicts, a good approach can be to use the Operational Transformation algorithm. In this algorithm, two operations O_1 and O_2 are transformed in such a way that both achieve the desired effect even when applied simultaneously.

4. Resilient Against Failures:

To prevent any data loss, we can replicate the file data into multiple copies across different data centers. Further, we can use Global Transaction Identifier to ensure Atomicity and Consistency across various Write operations.

Conclusion There is a lot that goes into designing a large-scale distributed system like Google Drive and many trade-offs to consider. This is just one such design with a few possible trade-offs.

Keep in mind that designs can differ based on the specific use-cases and assumptions being made, and this is a high level, simplified design.

10.3 Can you design a web search engine like Google?

Designing a web search engine like Google is a complex task that involves multiple components such as a web crawler, an indexer, and a query processor, among others.

1. **Web Crawler**: A crawler, also known as a spider or bot, is a program that browses the web in a methodical and automated manner. This process is called web crawling or spidering.

A web crawler starts with a list of URLs to visit, called the seeds. As the crawler visits these URLs, it identifies all the hyperlinks in the page and adds them to the list of URLs to visit. URLs from the frontier are recursively visited according to a set of policies. If the crawler is performing archiving of websites it copies and saves the information as it goes.

The basic algorithm for a web crawler is as follows:

```
procedure WebCrawler(SeedUrl)
    add SeedUrl to the frontier
    while frontier is not empty
        Url = get URL from frontier
        contents = fetch(Url)
        add Url to visited URLs list
        for all links in contents
            if link is not in visited URLs list
                add link to frontier
```

2. **Indexer**: After the web crawler has retrieved the pages, they need to be processed and indexed.

First, the page content is transformed - this could involve removing HTML tags, JavaScript, CSS and any other unnecessary content.

Then, the remaining text is tokenized, i.e., split into individual words, and these words are processed (e.g., case folding, stemming).

Finally, the tidied-up content is added to the index. An index might often be implemented as an inverted index, a data structure storing a mapping from content, such as words or numbers, to its locations in a document or a set of documents.

3. **Query Processor**: This is the component that processes user's search queries against the index and returns a list of results.

The query processor might analyze the user's input (e.g., parsing the query, apply synonyms), and then it will use the index to find relevant documents. The list of documents is then ranked based on various factors (e.g., content of page, PageRank).

Google uses a ranking algorithm called PageRank, which is calculated like this:

```
PR(A) = (1-d) + d (PR(T1)/C(T1) + ... + PR(Tn)/C(Tn))
```

where:

- 'PR(A)' is the PageRank of page A
- 'PR(Ti)' is the PageRank of pages Ti which link to page A
- 'C(Ti)' is the number of outbound links on page Ti
- 'd' is a damping factor which can be set between 0 and 1.

Designing and implementing a search engine is a very complex task and requires good understanding of various algorithms and data structures. This answer can just give a glimpse into the main concepts involved in a simplified manner.

10.4 How would you design a social network like Facebook?

Designing a social network like Facebook is a broad and multifaceted task, covering areas from back-end infrastructure to front-end interactivity. Here's one possible approach, focusing on the key components: data modeling, infrastructure, storage, search functionality and security.

1. **Data Modeling**

The users and their interactions are the core elements of any social network. The user-related data usually includes profile information, friends list, posts, photos, likes, shares, comments, etc. This is where graph databases (like Neo4j) can be highly beneficial due to their nature of representing and storing data in terms of nodes (representing users), edges (representing relationships), and properties (additional user-related information).

2. **Infrastructure**

The infrastructure should be built to be scalable and capable of efficient data processing. Microservices-based architecture is likely a good choice for this to ensure that each service can scale independently.

3. **Storage**

Given the large volumes of data typically involved in social networks, we need an efficient storage solution. This comprises:

a. **Database**: As mentioned earlier, a graph database can be ideal for handling user-related information. A NoSQL database could also be beneficial for handling semi-structured or unstructured data.

b. **File Storage**: Photos, videos, and other multimedia will require a robust and efficient file storage system. This could be achieved with a distributed file system such as Hadoop HDFS or a cloud file storage.

4. **Search Functionality**

Users should be able to search for people, posts, videos, etc. ElasticSearch, which is a highly scalable open-source full-text search and analytics engine can power this functionality. It allows users to perform and combine many types of searches.

5. **Security**

Security is crucial in a social network. User data should be encrypted, and the exchange of data must be securely done over HTTPS. User authentication could be handled by OAuth2.0 or OpenID.

Let's also discuss **News Feed Generation**, another important aspect of a Facebook-like social network.

A straightforward approach to news feed generation is to fetch the latest posts from all the users that a specific user follows. The data model might look like this:

```
User {
  userId,
  name,
  email,
  ...
}

Post {
  postId,
  userId,
  content,
  timestamp,
  ...
}

FeedItem {
  userId,
  postId,
  timestamp
}
```

Whenever a user makes a new post, a new feed item gets created for each of the user's followers with a reference to the post. Then, to fetch a user's news feed, fetch the latest 'N' posts in 'FeedItem' for that user and join on 'Post' to get post details.

Although simple, this approach might not scale well due to excessive write operations as the followers count increases. Thus, Facebook uses an algorithm (EdgeRank), prioritizing posts based on users' connection strength, the post's recency, and the kind of interaction.

This quick overview illustrates some of the foundations on which we could start to build. Each point could be expanded with much greater detail, and many more aspects (UX/UI, analytics, testing, etc.) would have to be addressed for a complete network.

10.5 How would you design a messaging app like WhatsApp?

Designing an application as large and complex as WhatsApp requires consideration of several important features and functionalities. Here, we will provide a high-level overview of the design process, though keep in mind that this is a simplified version and real-world applications would involve many more details, considerations and likely have architectural variations. For the sake of keeping things manageable, we will focus on some essential aspects of WhatsApp:

- User login and registration

- Contact list

- Real-time messaging (one-to-one and group chat)

- Delivery receipts

- Online/Offline status of users

- Multimedia messages

Now, let's look into each component one by one.

1) **User login and registration**

User authentication is typically achieved through a combination of username and password or through access tokens for third-party services like Google, Facebook, Twitter. Passwords should never be saved directly in the database. Instead, we should save hashed + salted passwords. A common approach is to use a cryptographic hash function (like Bcrypt).

2) **Contact List**

For storing users contact information, we would likely use a SQL database that would allow to store data in tables. The structure might be something like this:

```
Users
| User\_ID | User\_Name | Contact\_Info | ... |
-----------------------------------------------
| ...      | ...        | ...          | ... |

Contacts
| User\_ID | Contact\_ID |
------------------------
| ...      | ...        |
```

3) **Real-time messaging (one-to-one and group chat)**

WebSockets can be used for real-time bidirectional communication between the server (backend) and the client (User's device). This comes as an alternative to the traditional frequent polling of the server for updates, leading to efficient real-time updates.

For handling the messages, they can be stored in a SQL database:

```
Messages
```

```
| Message\_ID | User\_ID | TimeStamp | Text |
---------------------------------------------
|  ...        |  ...     |  ...      |  ... |
```

4) **Delivery Receipts**

This system should have a way to track if the message has been
sent, delivered, and seen. This can be achieved by adding more
columns to the Messages table in our database, specifying the
status of each message.

5) **Online/Offline status of users**

To maintain online and offline status, we can use a simple approach where whenever a user logs in, we update his/her status
as 'Online' in the database. Similarly, we can update 'Offline'
status when the user logs off.

6) **Multimedia messages**

For multimedia messages (images, videos, etc.), it would be
preferable to use a Blob Storage system or an object storage
service like Amazon S3, rather than attempting to store them
as BLOBs in a SQL database. The links to these objects can
be stored in the database similar to text messages.

This overview includes basic functionalities. It doesn't cover
additional important nuances like database sharding, system
scalability, push notifications, data encryption for security/pri-
vacy, location sharing, etc. which are significant for a complete
app like WhatsApp.

Also, remember to use DevOps (Development Operations) and
CI/CD(Continuous Integration and Continuous Delivery) during development and deployment for smoother operations and

faster production rates. In terms of technology stack, it could vary widely but some options would include Java or Kotlin for Android, Swift for iOS, Node.js or Python for backend, PostgreSQL or MongoDB for database, AWS or Google Cloud for hosting and storage services.

10.6 Can you design an online multiplayer game like Chess?

Designing an online multiplayer game like Chess involves multiple elements such as the game server, game client, networking, each player's interface, game rules, etc. For simplicity, let's discuss a form of the client-server model, a common architecture for online multiplayer games. The server will handle game rules, matchmaking, storing game state, etc. In this case, each player's client will be mostly responsible for graphical representation and interaction.

Here is a simple breakdown of the architecture:

1. Game Server:

The game server is a central place where all commands/actions from the player clients are processed and the updated state of the game is stored. In the case of chess, the server would process moves, check if they're valid according to the rules, update the game board state, and send updates to each client. The server could be implemented in languages such as C++, Java, Python, or NodeJS depending on your resources and requirements.

2. Game Client:

Each player interacts with the game through a client. The clients send player actions to the server (like moving a piece) and render the updated state of the game on their screens. Clients could be web-based or standalone applications depending on your player base. For a web-based client, HTML/CSS for the visual aspect, JavaScript for functionality, and WebSocket for real-time communication with the server could be used.

The client-server communication could look like this:

- The client sends a JSON object in the form of a string through WebSocket:

$$\{"action" : "move", "piece" : "E2", "destination" : "E4"\}$$

- The server processes the command, updates the game state, and sends a similar JSON object to both clients to represent the new state of the game board.

3. Database:

The database will store user information, game history, rankings, and other data. It might communicate directly with the game server for operations such as fetching and updating data. SQL or NoSQL databases could be used here, depending on the requirement.

Throughout the game, you might handle things a little differently for a "turn-based" game such as chess, where you don't necessarily need to have continuous updates from the server since the game state only changes when a player makes a move. The client would only need to send data to the server when a player makes a move, and the server would only need to send data to the clients when the move changes the game state (which in chess, is every move).

Additionally, don't forget to implement matchmaking logic on your server. If it's a 2-player game like chess, the server needs to pair two players who are looking for a game. Random pairing might be the simplest way to achieve this but for a competitive play you should implement a more complex system like the Elo rating formula.

Remember, much of this design would allow for a working but simple chess game. For a production game, many more factors would need to be taken into consideration, like security, performance, scalability, etc. This schema can act as a proof-of-concept to further advance upon.

10.7 How would you design a distributed cache?

Designing a distributed cache involves multiple considerations including consistent hashing, scalability, master-slave architecture, maintaining the replication factor, and ensuring fault tolerance.

1. **Consistent Hashing**: In a distributed cache system, many servers might be setup to cache incoming requests. One primary task is to decide which server will cache which request. A popular technique to decide this is to use consistent hashing.

Consistent hashing is a way to assign keys to nodes in such a way that when nodes are added or removed, only a minimal amount of key reassignments happen. In other words, it ensures that addition or removal of one node only affects the keys of that node and doesn't affect the keys in other nodes. This is done by creating a hash ring where each node gets a position on the ring based on its hashed value.

When a key needs to be found in the cache, it is hashed and found on the ring. If a node has failed, the key will be found at the next node in the ring.

2. **Scalability**: Scalability is paramount in distributed caching as it should be possible to scale the number of servers up or down according to demand. This can be achieved by adding more servers to the hash ring of a consistent hashing algorithm.

3. **Master-Slave Architecture**: A master-slave architecture can be used to avoid single point of failure. In this setup, all the write operations go to the master node which then replicates the data to its slave nodes. Read operations can go to any of the master node or the slave nodes. This architecture provides load balancing and redundancy.

4. **Maintaining the Replication Factor**: Since caches are not a reliable data store, data is usually replicated across multiple cache servers to ensure that it is available even if one of the cache servers goes down. Setting up the replication factor might depend on the trade-off between cost and reliability that a system is willing to maintain.

5. **Fault Tolerance**: To make the system more reliable, the cache servers may keep a backup of the data in a persistent store. This data is only accessed when it's not available in any of the cache servers. One of the cache servers will be responsible to keep this data synced with the cache.

The process for adding new servers, caching data, and fetching data is fairly linear:

- New servers are hashed and placed on the hash ring.

- Incoming data or request is hashed and assigned to a cache server based on the hash ring.

- When looking for data, if data is not available in the assigned server, the system moves in the clockwise direction on the hash ring to find an available server containing the data.

10.8 Can you design a recommendation system like the ones used on Amazon or Netflix?

Designing a recommendation system is quite a comprehensive task, requiring a deep understanding of various machine learning algorithms and techniques. However, for the sake of a high-level understanding, we'll dive into the foundations of creating a recommendation system similar to the ones used by companies like Amazon or Netflix.

Overview

There are mainly three types of recommendation systems:

1. **Collaborative Filtering:** This method makes automatic predictions (filtering) about the interest of a user by collecting preferences from many users (collaborating).

2. **Content-Based Filtering:** This method uses only information about the description and attributes of the items users has previously consumed to model user's preferences.

3. **Hybrid approaches:** These methods combine collaborative and content-based filtering. Hybrid approaches can be implemented in several ways: by making content-based and collaborative-based predictions separately and then combining them; by adding content-based capabilities to a collaborative-based approach (and vice versa);

or by unifying the approaches into one model.

Let's discuss each one of them in detail.

1. Collaborative Filtering

This method relies on the user's past behavior, like pages viewed, products bought, reviews given, etc., to find similarities between the users and make recommendations. It uses below two approaches:

- **User-User Collaborative Filtering (User-based approach):** This approach finds the users that are similar to the predicted user and recommend items that those similar users have liked before. Following is the cosine similarity formula that we can use to find the similarity between the users:

$$similarity(u, v) = \cos(\Theta) = \frac{u \cdot v}{||u||_2 * ||v||_2}$$

where u and v are two users.

- **Item-Item Collaborative Filtering (Item-based approach):** Instead of finding user's look-alike, it tries to find item's look-alike. Once the items look-alike of the target item (say, we need to find recommendations of item i), then items which are similar to item i, will be recommended.

Similarity between items 'm' and 'n' can also be calculated using cosine similarity, replacing user vectors with item vectors.

These similarity measures are then used to predict the ratings of the items that are not yet rated by a user, and finally recommending the top-N items with the highest predicted ratings.

2. Content-Based Filtering

This method uses meta-data such as genre, producer, actor, musician to recommend items say movies or music. This algorithm believes that if a person liked a particular item, he will also like similar items. Mathematically the algorithm will calculate the cosine similarity based on these meta-data.

3. Hybrid approaches

As the name suggests it's a mix of the above two. Why mix? Because it helps to alleviate the issues found in single approaches. For example, the similarity-based collaborative method suffers a problem known as the cold-start, where a new user or a new item arriving in the system can't be recommended until the user rates several items or the item gets rated by many users. This problem could be solved by using some content-based filtering.

Each of these approaches has its own strengths and weaknesses. Most of the recommendation systems in the industry are hybrids of the two methods.

Recommendation systems are a very broad field in machine learning and the details involve much more complex situations and algorithms, but hopefully, this answer provides a clear understanding of how to design one.

10.9   How would you design a rate limiter for a distributed system?

Designing a rate limiter for a distributed system can be challenging due to requirements such as scalability, fault-tolerance, and synchronization. Several methods can be used depending on the context and use cases. Here we discuss three common concepts used in designing rate limiters.

1. **Fixed Window Algorithm:**

The fixed window algorithm divides the time into equal size windows and allows only certain number of requests per window. If the limit is exceeded, subsequent requests are blocked until the next window.

Counter algorithm pseudocode:

```
If RequestTime > WindowEnd
    RequestCount = 1
    WindowEnd = RequestTime + WindowSize
Else
    If RequestCount > RateLimit
        Block Request
    Else
        RequestCount++
```

But it has a problem called burst traffic due to the synchronized requests after each window.

2. **Sliding Window Log Algorithm:**

Sliding window log algorithm solves the problem in the fixed window by logging each request's timestamp. It ensures that the count of requests within any given window size does not exceed the limit. But it requires large storage to save logs individually.

Sliding log pseudocode:

```
Log[RequestTime] = Request
Remove logs older than WindowSize from Log[RequestTime]
If Sizeof(Log) > RateLimit
    Block Request
```

3. **Token Bucket Algorithm:**

In this algorithm, a token is added to the bucket at every 1/rate time interval until it hits the capacity. When a request comes in, a token is removed if possible. If not, the request is blocked/waited until next token comes in.

Token bucket pseudocode:

```
At every 1/rate interval, Do
   If TokenCount < Capacity
      TokenCount++
Every Request, Do
   If TokenCount > 0
      TokenCount--
   Else
      Block/Wait the Request
```

In a distributed system, these algorithms need to be modified slightly due to concurrency issues. For example:

- A global counter/token-bucket can be implemented using a distributed lock to prevent race conditions.

- It can also be implemented locally on every machine and use a consensus protocol for synchronization. But the real-time hard limit cannot be guaranteed.

- Distributed logging system like Apache Kafka can be used for Sliding Window Log algorithm where timestamps are saved into the log in a distributed and fault-tolerant manner.

Use of a centralized key-value database store (for example, Redis) can also provide a solution. Two scenarios where Redis can be used efficiently:

- With Redis, you can model fixed window rate limiter using simple Redis commands combined with Lua script to make the operation atomic.

- For the sliding window rate limiter, the Sorted Sets data structure in Redis can be used.

Overall, each method has its advantages and trade-offs. It is essential to understand the behavior of incoming request traffic, system capacity, and specific needs of the application that integrates this rate limiter to choose a suitable method.

10.10 Can you design a scalable notification service?

Designing a scalable notification service requires careful planning and engineering. Below is a high-level design overview of such a service.

Let's consider a service that needs to send notifications to both users' emails and phones. The goal should be to handle billions of notifications efficiently and so, the service needs to be highly available, fault-tolerant, and scalable.

Architecture Design

1) **Client:** This can be a web page, mobile application, other web services which needs to send notifiactions.

2) **Notification Service API:** Responsible for accepting requests from client. Typically, a RESTful API or a gRPC.

3) **Message Queue (MQ):** Processes messages asynchronously. This ensures the API rapidly responds back to client instead of keeping it waiting for processing. Kafka or RabbitMq can be used for this purpose.

4) **Notification Service:** Picks up notifications from MQ, does the processing and sends out notifications. It scales as per load because more workers can be added as load increases.

5) **Email/Message Gateways:** Interfaces to send emails and SMS messages.

The general flow involves the client sending a notification to the notification service API. The API then creates a message in the MQ with all necessary data. Notification service workers consume these messages and process them.

Here's a simple sketch of the architecture:

```
Client -----> Notification API -----> Message Queue ----->
     Notification service -----> Gateway
```

Database Design

We might need a database to store the notifications if we intend to keep track of sent notifications or if the notifications are not instantly processed. It's recommended to keep the database design as simple as possible to improve scalability. A NoSQL database like Cassandra would be a good choice because they scale well horizontally and are good for write-heavy workload.

The 'Notifications' table could have columns like 'notification_id', 'user_id', 'notification_type', 'notification_content', 'status', etc.

Scalability Considerations

1. **Horizontally scale the Notification services:** As load increases, we add more workers/servers to handle that load. This design de-couples the notification sending from the API layer, so the API service can rapidly respond to clients.

2. **Partition the Message queue:** Kafka provides seamless partitioning and RabbitMQ has similar mechanisms so that a high rate of notifications can be handled concurrently.

3. **Database Sharding:** If we decide to store notifications, the data can become huge. Hence, horizontal sharding of data is necessary. This involves breaking up one's database into smaller chunks, called "shards". Each shard is held on a separate database server instance, to spread load and the size of the dataset.

Overall, it's clear that designing a scalable notification service involves good architectural design, effective database use, and provisions to horizontally scale key components.

Chapter 11

Scaling, Data Partitioning, Load Balancing, Caching

11.1 How would you horizontally scale a system?

Scaling a system horizontally means to add more machines or nodes to a system to handle increased load. This approach is also known as "scale-out", and it forms a significant part of modern distributed systems.

Here are step-by-step ways to horizontally scale a system:

1. **Load Balancing:** Utilize a load balancer that distributes network or application traffic across many instances of your ap-

plication. Each individual instance doesn't have to be powerful, as increased load can be handled by adding more instances. The load balancer will distribute incoming requests to each instance evenly, which helps prevent any one instance from becoming a bottleneck. Examples of load balancing solutions include Nginx or Apache HTTP Server for software level and AWS Elastic Load Balancer for cloud level.

2. **Stateless Applications:** When scaling out, it's important to make sure the application is stateless on the server side. This means each request should not depend on the server's state or previous requests. This feature makes it possible to distribute requests to different instances, as they all reply with the same output when given the same input.

3. **Distributed Data Store:** When a system scales horizontally, data consistency becomes a challenge. Using a distributed data store like Amazon's DynamoDB or Google's Bigtable can ensure that data remains consistent across all instances of your application.

4. **Use of Distributed Caches:** To make your system more efficient in terms of reading data, you can use distributed caching systems like Memcached or Redis. They temporarily store data that's frequently accessed, reducing the read-load on your databases and making retrieval faster.

5. **Implementing an Auto-scaling Policy:** Implement an auto-scaling policy in order to add or reduce instances based on the demand. Especially with cloud computing, such as AWS, Google Cloud, or Azure, this technique can save costs and manage resources effectively. AWS Auto Scaling and Kubernetes' Horizontal Pod Autoscaler are examples of this.

6. **Partitioning** (also known as sharding): Split large databases
into smaller, faster, more easily managed parts called data
shards. The shards are spread across multiple servers. One
server can store multiple shards, and each shard can store table
rows.

For example, a database of online users can be sharded by the
user's geographic location: one shard can contain users from
America, another can contain users from Europe, and another
can contain users from Asia.

$$\text{User Database} = Shard\_\text{America} \cup Shard\_\text{Europe} \cup Shard\_\text{Asia}$$

Please keep in mind that the appropriate horizontal scaling
strategy might vary based on the specific requirements and constraints of the system in question.

11.2   What strategies would you use to par-
tition data?

Data partitioning is an integral part of database design that
deals with splitting your data into separate components or partitions to optimize querying, enhance performance, and improve
maintenance. Here are some popular strategies you can leverage
to partition data:

1. **Range Partitioning**: Here, datasets are divided depending on the range of their key value. Consider the following
example where we have employee data and we want to parti-

tion this data based on employee_id, which lies between 1 and 10000:

- Partition 1 : 1 <= employee_id < 2500
- Partition 2 : 2500 <= employee_id < 5000
- Partition 3 : 5000 <= employee_id < 7500
- Partition 4 : 7500 <= employee_id <= 10000

This approach is beneficial when the data features a significant distribution across a particular field.

2. **Hash Partitioning**: This method uses a hash function to partition data. It provides an evenly distributed partitioning, ensuring all partitions contain nearly the same amount of data. For example, we could use a hash function to distribute employee_id values across four partitions. If 'hash(employee_id) mod 4' yields 0,1,2, or 3, we place that data in corresponding partition 0,1,2, or 3.

3. **List Partitioning**: This involves partitioning data according to a list of values. Each partition is defined by a list of values. If a value matches an element in the list, it is stored in the corresponding partition. For example, if we want to partition employee data based on a predefined list of departments, we can create a separate partition for 'sales', 'marketing', 'finance', and 'HR'.

4. **Composite Partitioning**: Sometimes, the ways above may not suffice individually. You may need to use a blend of two methods, which is known as Composite Partitioning. Again, using the employee database, we can create a range partitioning using employee_id, and then each of these ranges can be further hash partitioned depending on departments.

5. **Round-robin Partitioning**: Simplest form of partitioning where data is distributed equally across all partitions in a circular manner. It doesn't take into consideration the data it is spreading across the partitions. This approach is beneficial when the data to be partitioned is expected to be evenly distributed.

One essential aspect to keep in mind while choosing the partitioning strategy is the data retrieval pattern. Partitioning should simplify data retrieval and improve performance. Consequently, it's essential to understand the data pattern, data distribution, and business use cases that would need data retrieval before choosing the data partitioning strategy.

Here is an example in Python of data partitioning using the Range Partitioning method:

```
def range_partition(data, range_indices):
    """Perform range partitioning on data.

    Arguments:
    data -- an input dataset which is a list
    range_indices -- the index list of ranges to be split

    Return:
    result -- the partitioned dataset which is a list of lists
    """
    result = []
    n_bin = len(range_indices)

    # For each bin, perform the following
    for i in range(n_bin):
        # Find elements to be belonging to each range
        s = [x for x in data if x < range_indices[i]]
        # Add the partitioned list to the result
        result.append(s)
        # Remove elements that have been partitioned from the
            original data
        data = [x for x in data if x >= range_indices[i]]

    # For the last partition, add all remaining data
    result.append([x for x in data if x >= range_indices[-1]])

    return result
```

Then call the function with:

```
# Define data
data = [8.5, 5.0, 10.2, 4.2, 5.5, 1.9, 8.7, 7.1, 6.3, 5.3]

# Define the range indices
range_indices = [5.0, 7.0, 9.0]

# Perform range partitioning
result = range_partition(data, range_indices)

# Print result
for i, s in enumerate(result):
    print(f'Partition {i}: {s}')
```

The output would be:

```
Partition 0: [4.2, 1.9]
Partition 1: [5.0, 5.5, 6.3, 5.3]
Partition 2: [8.5, 7.1]
Partition 3: [10.2, 8.7]
```

This would mean that data records have been partitioned among these four partitions based on their value.

11.3 How would you handle hot spots in your cache?

Hot spots in a cache are areas of high read/write activity that could potentially degrade the performance of a cache system. Handling these hot spots is an important part of cache optimization and can be approached in several ways:

1. **Horizontal Scaling:** This approach involves the addition of more nodes to the cache system. By distributing data across more nodes, the load can be balanced, reducing the impact of hot spots.

2. **Data Partitioning:** It involves splitting the data across different cache nodes, which could be base on a hash of the data key. This approach can limit the impact of a hot spot to a single partition rather than the entire cache.

3. **Replication:** If multiple clients are trying to read the same hot data item, the system can replicate the data item to multiple cache nodes. With each replica responsible for serving a subset of the clients, the request load can be evidently balanced. Keep in mind that although it works well for read-heavy workloads, replication may introduce complexity for write-heavy workloads, for instance, maintaining consistency would be challenging.

Example: Assuming we have two clients "A" and "B" both requesting for a data item "X". In a usual scenario, the request would be laid on one cache node only. But with replication, two cache nodes "Cache 1" and "Cache 2" store the same data item "X". The client "A" can read data from "Cache 1", and client "B" can read from "Cache 2". This reduces the load on a single node.

The math formulas for these concepts would involve calculating hash values for partitioning, or determining the number of nodes necessary for replication or scaling, which would depend on the specific systems and performance requirements involved.

The load distribution in horizontal scaling and data partitioning can be represented using the following bar chart.

Here the total number of requests is equally distributed among the cache nodes.

Cache Nodes	Number of Requests
Cache Node 1	100
Cache Node 2	100
Cache Node 3	100

4. **Use of Consistent Hashing:** This is another strategy used to deal with hotspots in cache. This type of hashing minimizes the reorganization of the hash table when a server is added or removed thus reducing the possible hotspots.

5. **Caching Algorithms:** Certain caching algorithms such as the Least Recently Used (LRU), Most Recently Used (MRU), or Least Frequently Used (LFU) can also help to prevent hot spots. These algorithms aim to discard the 'least useful' items first. For example, the LRU caching algorithm evicts the least recently used items first.

6. **Intelligent Load Balancing:** It involves analyzing and predicting the traffic patterns of incoming network traffic and distributing this traffic efficiently to resources to improve performance.

Keep in mind that the best approach may depend on the specific data and access patterns in your application. It's often best to monitor the cache's performance over time, make incremental changes, and continuously evaluate the results.

11.4   Can you describe the different types of load balancers and how they work?

Load balancers are technology designed to evenly distribute network or application traffic across a number of servers. The aim of this is to prevent any single server from becoming overworked, which could degrade performance. Load balancing improves responsiveness and increases the availability and reliability of applications.

There are different types of load balancers based on the method they use to direct network traffic, including:

1. **Round Robin**: Round Robin load balancing is one of the simplest methods for distributing client requests across a group of servers. When a request comes in, the round robin algorithm routes it to the next server in the list. The algorithm loops through the server list until it reaches the end. When it does, it starts again at the top. It decides the order of request processing based on a list or cyclic order.

Example: If there are 3 servers, the first request goes to Server 1, the second request to Server 2, the third request to Server 3, then the fourth request goes back to Server 1, and so on in a cyclical order.

2. **Least Connections**: In this method, the load balancer maintains a record of how many connections each server has. When a new request comes in, the load balancer routes the request to the server with the fewest connections.

Example: If Server 1 has 2 active connections, Server 2 has 3 active connections, and Server 3 has 1 active connection, the next client request would be sent to Server 3.

3. **IP Hash**: The IP Hash load balancing algorithm maps
IP addresses to the available servers. The load balancer creates
a unique hash key based on the client and server's IP addresses,
then assigns the connection to a server, relying on the key value.
This allows specific client IP addresses to always reach the same
server, as long as no change in server availability occurs.

With the IP Hash method, an IP address, say '192.165.1.2', is
hashed to a server. Even if this client goes offline and comes
back, it's still mapped to the same server.

4. **Least Response Time**: This method routes new requests
to the server with the fewest active connections and the lowest
average response time.

5. **URL Hash**: This load balancing method uses the hashes
of the URL requested by the user to determine which server will
handle the request. This is useful for balancing requests for
a specific set of URLs especially in a caching situation where
remaining consistent in which server the request goes to helps
improve caching efficiency.

The use of load balancers also implies the use of health checks
– mechanisms for the load balancer to know if a server is ready
to receive requests and respond in expected timing. If a server
fails health checks, typically the load balancer stops sending
traffic to the failing server.

By distributing the work evenly, load balancers prevent any
single server from becoming a bottleneck, thereby increasing
overall service availability and response times. Which type of
load balancer to employ depends largely on the nature of the

traffic and the specific needs of the application.

11.5 How would you decide between SQL and NoSQL?

Deciding between SQL and NoSQL comes down to the specific needs of your application. Here are some considerations that may guide the decision.

1. Data Structure:

* **SQL:** SQL databases are relational, meaning they organize data into tables. They are great if you need to ensure data integrity and you are dealing with complex queries. If your data structure fits nicely into a table, then you might want to use a SQL database.

* **NoSQL:** These databases are great for hierarchical data storage. They store data in a key-value pair method. It's a preferable choice when data is not structured or when the design of your data is not decided yet.

2. Scalability:

* **SQL:** SQL databases are vertically scalable, which means that you can increase the load on a single server by increasing things like CPU, RAM or SSD.

* **NoSQL:** NoSQL databases are horizontally scalable, which means that you handle more traffic by sharding, or adding more servers in your NoSQL database.

3. Complexity of Query:

* **SQL:** It's a better option if you have a complex query to run, as SQL databases are very good at that.

* **NoSQL:** Not the best option to run complex queries as they lack standard interfaces to the data and don't offer robust ad-hoc query capabilities.

4. ACID Properties (Atomicity, Consistency, Isolation, Durability):

* **SQL:** SQL databases follow all ACID properties. So, it's preferable when you need a high consistency in a data (like in banking systems).

* **NoSQL:** NoSQL is best when the data is not highly consistent, and ACID properties are not needed.

Example:

Consider the case where you are building a system for a library. For tracking the books, authors, borrowers and borrowing history, a SQL database would be a good fit, because the relationships between these entities are a good match for a relational database.

On the other hand, if you are capturing logs from a high-traffic website for analysis of user behavior, a NoSQL database might be a better fit because the volume of data is large, and relationships among the data are less important.

Comparison Chart:

| Feature | SQL | NoSQL |

```
|-----------------------|----------|-----------|
| Database Type         | Relational | Non-Relational |
| Scaling               | Vertical Scaling | Horizontal Scaling |
| Data Structure        | Table-based | Key-Value Pairs, wide-column stores,
                                      graph or document |
| Complex Queries       | Better | Not so good |
| ACID Compliance       | Yes | Not always |
| Atomic Updates        | Yes | Depends on specific database |
| Multi-record ACID transactions | Yes | No (except for a few) |
| Schema                | Pre-defined | Dynamic |
```

So, the choice between SQL and NoSQL should be based on the
specific needs of your system, whether you need ACID transactions, the complexity of your queries, and how you need your
database to scale.

11.6   How does a CDN work and why is it important?

A Content Delivery Network (CDN) is a geographically distributed group of servers that work together to provide fast
delivery of Internet content. It allows the quick transfer of as-
sets needed for loading Internet content including HTML pages,
JavaScript files, stylesheets, images, and videos. Because much
of today's Internet content is served through CDNs, they have
become a crucial part of the web infrastructure and have great
importance.

A primary reason CDNs are used is to reduce latency, the delay
that occurs from the moment you request to load a web page
to the moment its content actually appears onscreen. This process involves multiple network hops, and each hop introduces a
certain delay. Because the CDN's servers are closer to the user,

there's a good chance that the number of hops and therefore latency will be reduced.

Here's a brief overview on how CDN works:

1. **Content Storage and Delivery**: When a user makes a request to a website, instead of going all the way to the site's original server, CDN redirects the request to a copy of the website stored in a cache server that is geographically closer to the user.

2. **Caching**: CDN stores a cached version of its content in multiple geographical locations (known as points of presence, or PoPs). Each PoP contains a number of caching servers responsible for content delivery to visitors within its proximity.

3. **Service Nodes**: Each node (or edge server) in the CDN caches the content, so when a user request is made, the node closest to the user will serve the content, which drastically reduces latency and improves site speed.

CDN Importance:

1. **Improved User Experience**: CDN makes data fetching significantly faster and efficient, elevating the user experience.

2. **Scalability**: A CDN allows for easy scalability during times of high traffic to keep websites functioning smoothly.

3. **Security**: Beyond delivering content, most CDNs also offer security services like DDoS protection and secure socket layer (SSL) encryption to safeguard the sites from cyber threats.

4. **SEO**: Fast-loading websites are rewarded by search engines with higher positions in search results, thus improving

SEO for a website.

5. **Content Availability and Redundancy**: If one server
fails, CDN technology can easily redirect a user's request to
another available server.

This entire process can be summarized in one simple equation:

$$\text{User's total waiting time} = \frac{\text{Size of the requested resource}}{\text{Capacity of the communication channel}}$$
$$\times \text{ Distance between the user and the server delivering the resource}$$

As you can see, by decreasing the distance between the user and
the server (which a CDN does), you reduce the total waiting
time for resource delivery.

11.7 How would you handle data replication and consistency across multiple databases in different regions?

Handling data replication and consistency across multiple databases
in different regions is a complex task that involves a balance
between availability, consistency, and partition tolerance, as
dictated by the CAP theorem.

Let's break down the problem into two parts: replication and
consistency.

1. Replication: It refers to the sharing of information to ensure
consistency between redundant resources to improve reliability, fault-tolerance, or accessibility. This could be employing
techniques like:

a. Snapshot Replication: This involves copying and distributing data and database objects from one database to another. It then synchronizes the data on a scheduled basis.

b. Transactional Replication: This type of replication involves sharing of data across databases in almost real-time. Once the data is modified in the Master table, it's replicated across to its subscribers.

c. Merge Replication: This type of replication combines data from multiple sources into a single central database. This is more complex and is used in distributed systems.

d. Peer to Peer Replication: This involves multiple servers sharing the same level of importance, meaning no server is superior to another. As such, every change applied to one peer is propagated to all other nodes, ensuring high availability and load balancing.

2. Consistency: This ensures that a read operation will return the value of the most recent write operation to a certain data item. You may apply eventual or strong consistency models based on your software's requirements.

An approach to accomplish consistency in a distributed database could be through using consensus algorithms like PAXOS, Raft, and ZAB. These are designed to ensure system reliability and are essential to implement databases, message queues, and log systems.

Another approach could be implementing Multi-Master Replication where all databases are considered as a master, and any change on any master is asynchronously replicated to other peers.

However, maintaining consistency across large and geographically separated DB might affect performance. In many situations, one often elects to relax to eventual consistency for better availability and performance, as defined by CAP theorem.

CAP theorem, also known as Brewer's theorem, states that it is impossible for a distributed data store to simultaneously provide more than two out of the following three guarantees:

C - Consistency (all nodes see the same data at the same time)

A - Availability (a guarantee that every request receives a response about whether it succeeded or failed)

P - Partition tolerance (system continues to operate despite arbitrary partitioning due to network failures)

For any distributed system, one usually needs to choose between consistency and availability depending on the nature of the software.

Consistency Levels	Scenarios
Strong Consistency	Highly sensitive data (financial systems, health records)
Eventual Consistency	Real-time multi-player games, chat apps, collaborative docs

Final thoughts, handling data replication and consistency across multiple databases situated in different regions is crucial for high availability and fault tolerance of applications, but it has to be done carefully to avoid a performance bottleneck.

11.8   How does a database index work and why is it important?

A database index is a data structure that improves the speed of data retrieval operations on a database table. It works in a similar way to an index in a book: instead of scanning the entire book to find a particular topic, you can go to the index, find the topic, and then go directly to the pages that contain this topic.

Let's assume a phone book with thousands of names and phone numbers. If you were tasked to find the phone number of a particular person, the brute force method would be to start from the first page and flip through each subsequent page until you find the person. However, if the phone book has an index, you can directly go to the page where the person's details are recorded, thus saving a lot of time.

In databases, indices work similarly. Suppose we have a 'Customers' table in a database and we regularly need to find customers based on their 'CustomerID'. Without an index on 'CustomerID', the database engine would need to look at each row in the Customers table to find a particular 'CustomerID' (this is known as a full table scan), which can be very slow if there are many customers. However, with an index on 'CustomerID', the database engine can quickly find the row for a particular 'CustomerID' without needing to look at every row.

Indices can also be made on multiple columns, known as composite index. For example, if an application often needs to look up customers by 'LastName' and 'FirstName' together, then a composite index on ('LastName', 'FirstName') would speed up these lookups.

However, there's a trade-off while using indexing. While it speeds up data retrieval, it slows down data insertion, update, and deletion. This is because every time data is changed, the index also needs to be updated.

Generally speaking, the database engine uses a B-tree data structure for indexes. A B-tree keeps data sorted and allows searches, insertions, and deletions in logarithmic time.

The diagram of a simple B-tree index on 'CustomerID' might look something like this:

```
    15
   /  \
 10    20
```

Here, each node represents a page on disk where a certain range of 'CustomerIDs' are stored. The root node says that 'CustomerIDs' less than 15 are on the left and 'CustomerIDs' greater than or equal to 15 are on the right. Then each subsequent node tells you which disk page to look at, until you arrive at the leaf node that holds the 'CustomerID'.

So, creating the appropriate indices can greatly speed up data retrieval, but they should be used judiciously, considering the nature of operations performed on the database and the size of the tables.

11.9 How would you implement caching strategies to improve performance?

Caching can be an efficient way to enhance the performance and responsiveness of your applications by storing frequently accessed data in memory to prevent time-consuming operations, such as database SQL queries or computing complex calculations. There are several caching strategies, and the implementation will depend on the specific needs and constraints of your system. Here are some of the most popular caching strategies:

1. Least Recently Used (LRU):

In an LRU caching scheme, the system removes the least recently used items first. This strategy requires keeping track of what was used when, which is expensive if your cache is large.

Here is a pseudo code example:

```
class LRUCache:

    def __init__(self, capacity):
        self.cache = OrderedDict()
        self.capacity = capacity

    def get(self, key):
        if key not in self.cache:
            return -1
        self.cache.move_to_end(key)
        return self.cache[key]

    def put(self, key, value):
        if key in self.cache:
            self.cache.move_to_end(key)
        self.cache[key] = value
        if len(self.cache) > self.capacity:
            self.cache.popitem(last=False)
```

In this code, the ordered dictionary keeps track of the order of operations (insertion order by default). When a new pair

is inserted, it's added to the end of the cache. If the cache
exceeds its capacity, the pair at the front of the cache (i.e., the
least recently used one) is evicted.

2. Time to Live (TTL):

TTL is a method where a value (time in seconds) is associated with every cache record. When the record is requested,
the application checks if the current time is beyond the stored
timestamp+TTL. If it is, the record is not used, and the data
source is queried (and the cache record is optionally recreated
for future use).

3. Least Frequently Used (LFU):

In this caching scheme, the system removes the least frequently
used items first. Particular attention needs to be paid to items
used with the same frequency, for which an additional "recency"
discriminator might be necessary.

A pseudo code of LFU with recency factor would look something
like this:

```
class LFUCache:

    def __init__(self, capacity):
        self.capacity = capacity
        self.cache = {} # key:val
        self.frequency = {} # key: [frequency, recency]
        self.recency = 0

    def get(self, key):
        if key in self.cache:
            self.frequency[key][0] += 1
            self.frequency[key][1] = self.recency
            self.recency += 1
            return self.cache[key]
        return -1

    def put(self, key, val):
        if len(self.cache) == self.capacity:
            lfu = min(self.frequency.keys(), key=lambda k:self.
                frequency[k])
```

```
      del self.cache[lfu]
        del self.frequency[lfu]
    self.cache[key] = val
    self.frequency[key] = [1, self.recency]
    self.recency += 1
```

In the code above, we maintain two maps, one for the cache
that maps a key to a value, and another for the frequencies of
the keys. The frequency map actually stores a list against each
key - the first element being the frequency itself, and the second
one being the recency factor (which is the simple increasing time
from when elements were accessed or put).

Note: The performance of LFU and LRU as cache eviction
policies over others, such as First In, First Out (FIFO), largely
depends on the specifics of the workload at hand. In most
general cases, though, LFU and LRU tend to perform quite
well.

11.10 What are the considerations when choosing between strong and eventual consistency?

Choosing between strong and eventual consistency in a distributed system has significant implications for your application's performance, functionality, and user experience. Here
are some considerations:

1. **Data Integrity**: Strong consistency guarantees that every read receives the most recent write. This means that all
clients see the same data at the same time, eliminating am-
biguity. It's essential in systems where you need a source

of truth such as financial systems and OTT (Over The Top) applications. To contrast, eventual consistency allows temporary inconsistencies and guarantees that updates will propagate through the system given some time.

Use a banking application as an example. With strong consistency, if User A transfers money to User B, both of them see the transfer immediately. But with eventual consistency, User B may not see the transferred amount instantly.

2. **Latency**: Strong consistency often leads to higher latency as it may need to reach a consensus among nodes before it can return a result. Contrarily, eventual consistency can provide low-latency responses as it can return a result without having to write to all replicas. This is especially useful in systems where the speed of accessing data is more critical than seeing the most recent data.

For example, if you were designing a comments system for a busy blog site, eventual consistency may be preferred. It may not be a disaster if some users don't see a new comment for a short while, but it is essential that the site can quickly serve many parallel requests.

3. **Availability**: According to the CAP theorem, it's impossible for a distributed data store to simultaneously provide more than two out of the following three guarantees: Consistency, Availability, and Partition Tolerance. In an event of a network partition, systems that choose to be consistent will have to refuse operations, whereas systems that choose eventual consistency can stay available and handle operations. Hence, if high availability is a high priority, then eventual consistency should be preferred like in social media applications.

4. **Operational Overhead and Complexity**: Implementing strong consistency requires a more complex algorithm, which adds to developmental and operational overhead. In return, it eases reasoning about the system behavior. Eventual consistency is operationally simpler but demands application design to handle inconsistent states.

To formalize the tradeoffs:

With strong consistency,

$$C > L, A$$

(C: Consistency, L: Latency, A: Availability)

With eventual consistency,

$$L, A > C$$

In conclusion, There is no "one size fits all". The choice between strong and eventual consistency depends on the type of application, the specific use case, and the tolerable trade-offs.

Chapter 12

Designing Real-World Systems

12.1 Can you design a distributed logging system for a cloud infrastructure?

Designing a distributed logging system for a cloud infrastructure involves several components and requires careful consideration of the goals of the system. The system should be robust, efficient, scalable and should allow for effective log analysis. Let's look at a simple design for such a system:

Components of System

1. **Agent/Logger**: This is installed on each machine (or within each application) and is responsible for collecting and sending logs to the next component. The logger can collect logs in various ways such as file logs, system logs or through

application APIs.

2. **Transport Layer**: This is a message queuing service like Kafka or RabbitMQ that acts as a buffer which takes logs from agents and sends it to central storage. These services can handle massive throughput while ensuring resilient and loss-tolerant communication.

3. **Central Storage/Log Aggregator**: This is responsible for receiving logs from all machines/instances and storing them efficiently for future uses. Solutions like Elasticsearch or Amazon S3 can be used. For more real-time analysis Elasticsearch would be more suitable due to its powerful search capabilities.

4. **Indexer**: It is used to index the incoming data to make it searchable. Elasticsearch has the built-in capability to perform indexing.

5. **Analytics or Visualizer**: This is responsible for analyzing the logs for troubleshooting, auditing, monitoring, or anomaly detection. Kibana or Grafana are examples of good visualization tools.

Roughly the system looks like this: "' Logger/Agent -> Transport Layer/Message Bus -> Log Aggregator -> Indexer -> Analyzer "'

Design points to note

1. **Reliability and Data loss:** The system must be robust enough to handle failures at each point and replicate data to avoid loss. Kafka, for instance, takes care of this at the transport layer with its fault-tolerant storage system.

2. **Scalability:** The system should be equally capable of

handling a small number of logs and scaling up to handle an increase in volume. This requires consideration at each point, such as horizontal scalability at the storage and transport layers.

3. **Uniform data representation:** Logs can come in different formats and need to be put in a format that can be uniformly readable and analyzable. JSON is widely accepted for this due to its easy-to-use and readable format.

4. **Security:** Logs can contain sensitive data so encryption while at rest and in transit along with access controls is vital.

5. **Real-time Analysis and Alerting:** Time-critical applications require real-time monitoring and you want to get alerted when there are critical issues.

A sample log from such a system might look like this:

```
{
  "timestamp": "2022-01-01T00:00:10Z",
  "level": "ERROR",
  "message": "Failed to connect to database",
  "service_id": "service-101",
  "machine_id": "machine-205"
}
```

This log indicates that at the given timestamp, the system failed to connect to the database, the error occurred at service-101 running on machine-205.

Please remember this is a very simplified example, a real-world application would require considering a lot more complexities including but not limited to, handling high logging throughput, eliminating duplicate logs, and more robust fault-tolerance.

12.2   How would you design a real-time comment system like Reddit or Quora?

Designing a real-time comment system involves various components including database architecture, caching, APIs, real-time messaging, and notification service. Here's a high-level design:

Database Design:

We can use a relational DB like SQL or a NoSQL DB like MongoDB as per our requirements.

- User: UserId (Primary Key), Name, Email, Password
- Post: PostId (Primary Key), Body, CreatedAt, UserId (Foreign Key)
- Comment: CommentId (Primary Key), Body, CreatedAt, UserId (Foreign Key), PostId (Foreign Key)
- Reply: ReplyId (Primary Key), Body, CreatedAt, UserId (Foreign Key), CommentId (Foreign Key)

Caching:

To reduce database load, we could use a caching system like Redis. Frequently accessed data could be cached and data that changes often will be updated in the cache and the database.

APIs:

- 'createComment': To submit a new Comment.
- 'editComment': To edit an existing Comment.
- 'deleteComment': To delete a Comment.
- 'getComments': To retrieve Comments for a Post, might include

pagination.

Real-time Commenting and Notification System:

For real-time commenting, WebSocket can be used. WebSocket provides bidirectional communication between the server and the client. Whenever a new update is available, it is directly pushed to the connected clients.

Scaling:

To handle large-scale data, horizontal scaling (sharding the database) could be introduced. Load balancers can be used for distributing traffic.

Now, let's discuss some additional optimization and scaling techniques.

1. Database Denormalization & Indexing:

Database queries could be slow if there are millions of comments on a post. To handle this, we can denormalize our database and keep the count of comments and recent comments data with the post info.

```
Post: PostId, Body, CreatedAt, UserId, CommentCount, RecentComments
```

Indexing on PostId, CommentedAt, and UserId columns will make our queries faster.

2. Sharding:

We can distribute our data across multiple databases based on PostId. We can use Consistent Hashing for distribution. Hence, if a new shard is added or an existing one is removed, we only need to reorganize a minimal amount of data.

3. Caching of Top or Trending Posts/Comments:

Frequently accessed posts/comments should be cached. While generating the news feed, we can check in the cache if the top/trending posts are available - if so, serve from cache, else query the DB and store it in the cache for future requests.

4. Load Balancing:

Load balancing should be used to distribute the network traffic across multiple servers. We can leverage Round Robin, Least connections or IP Hash methods for distribution. In the case of web socket servers, Sticky sessions should be used to ensure a user is always directed to the same server he opened a socket connection with.

The above suggestions form a high-level design of the system and can be further detailed and optimized based on specific use cases or requirements.

12.3 How would you design a system to efficiently compute rank on a high frequency basis, like a leaderboard system in games?

Designing a system for high frequency rank computation such as a leaderboard system in gaming involves dealing with lots of real-time data. The right choice of data structure and correct usage of caching and indexing are crucial in such a scenario.

Key points to consider:

1. Real Time Update: The data needs to update in real time as it is a gaming environment.

2. Data Scaling: With an increasing number of players and games, the data handling should scale proportionally.

Here's a suggestion on how to design such a system:

1. **Data Structure:**

To handle the data, a Binary Search Tree (BST) would be fit. In BSTs, each node contains players with score less than itself in the left subtree and with score bigger than itself in the right subtree.

Let's assume the BST holds players where each node is: $[player_{ID}, player_{Score}, Rank, left_{SubTreeSize}, right_{SubTreeSize}]$; the data structure itself will intrinsically have the ranking information.

2. **Real-Time Update:**

Any time a player's score updates, we delete that player's node and reinsert the node with the new score. To ensure the process is efficient, we need to maintain a Hash Map which will map $player_{ID}$ to the respective TreeNode.

3. **Rank Calculation:**

Once the BST is ready, you can compute the rank of a player in O(log n) time. When you search for a player (starting at the root), at each node:

- If the node score is equal to the player score, return the size of right subtree + 1 (Rank starts from 1 and not 0)

- If the node score is greater than the player score, go left in the tree 1. If the node score is less than the player score, go right and add the size of the right subtree along with the root; to a RankCounter.

Furthermore, consider the following:

4. **Use of Caching:**

Cache the top players and ranks so that it doesn't need to compute again and again. This will reduce the computation time drastically.

5. **Database and Indexing:**

Use a database like MongoDB to store player scores and their data. Use indexing on scores to make the operation faster.

6. **Concurrency Controls:**

As it's a high frequency system, there should be appropriate locks in place to handle multiple players updating their scores at the same time.

Note: This solution assumes scores are unique for simplicity. If the scores are not unique, each node of the BST can be modified to store a list of players with the same score, or use some kind of tie-breaking rule.

12.4 Can you design a ride-sharing service like Uber?

Designing a ride-sharing service like Uber involves several components, each requiring different expertise from computer science and software engineering. The basic components are:

1. User application

2. Driver application

3. Server

Let's try to design this system in a simplified form:

User Application:

This is the app users use to find a ride. Here are some key features:

1. **Request a ride**: The user enters their current location and destination. Locations can be a pre-defined list or input via map.

2. **Matching with drivers**: Once the locations are entered, the system performs spatial search to find nearby drivers.

3. **Price estimation**: It calculates an estimate of the ride cost based on distance, surge pricing, etc.

4. **Tracking the driver**: It shows the real-time location of the driver.

5. **Payment**: It handles the ride payment at the end.

Driver Application:

This is the app used by drivers. Key features include:

1. **Availability status**: The drivers can set their availability status.

2. **Ride acceptance**: It shows the incoming ride requests and lets the driver accept or reject.

3. **Navigation**: It shows route to pick up point and destination.

Server:

This is where all the processing happens. Key features include:

1. **Matching algorithms**: Using geospatial algorithms (like k-d trees or R-tree) to match user's ride requests with nearby available drivers.

2. **Price calculation**: Uses factors like demand-supply ratio (for surge), base price, distance, etc. to calculate trip cost.

3. **Real-time tracking**: It handles real-time updates of driver's location.

4. **Payment processing**: It handles the transaction between user and driver.

The system can be represented with the following diagram:

```
graph RL
  A((User))
  B((Server/Database))
  C((Driver))
  A -->|Request Ride| B
  B -->|Find nearest driver| C
  C -->|Accept/Decline| B
  B -->|Update User| A
  A -->|Complete Ride and Pay| B
  B -->|Update Driver| C
```

Here's the pseudo-code to handle a ride request:

```
function handleRideRequest(userLocation, destination):
  nearestDrivers = queryNearestDrivers(userLocation)
  if not nearestDrivers:
    return "No drivers available"
```

```
ride = createRide(userLocation, destination)
for driver in nearestDrivers:
  if sendRideRequest(driver, ride):
    startRealTimeTracking(driver)
    return "Ride␣is␣on␣the␣way"

return "No␣drivers␣accepted␣the␣ride"
```

This is a high-level design of the system. Design considerations can get very complex when we take into account real-world implications, like traffic, high demand periods, huge number of users and drivers, etc.

The complexity of these systems is the reason why companies like Uber have large engineering teams and still face engineering and infrastructure challenges.

12.5 How would you design an email delivery system that can ensure email delivery with high availability?

Designing an email delivery system with high availability requires thinking about several key areas including system architecture, data replication, load balancing, failover strategies and monitoring. Here's a general design process:

1. **System Architecture**:

We should adopt a distributed microservice-based architecture. In this design, distinct components of the service, such as the SMTP servers, email processing services, and frontend servers, can all be scaled out separately and updated independently without affecting the entire system.

2. **Data Replication and Redundancy**:

To ensure availability, you need to protect against single points of failure. Use redundant storage and data replication strategies to ensure there are always multiple copies of your data. A common strategy is to use an eventually consistent data store like Apache Cassandra, which provides tunable consistency and high availability, or Google Cloud's Spanner, which provides strong global consistency.

3. **Load Balancing**:

Load balancing helps your system to manage traffic efficiently. Load balancers can distribute the incoming emails across multiple SMTP servers to prevent any single server from becoming a bottleneck. There are many types of load balancing algorithms available such as Round Robin, Weighted Round Robin, Least Connection, etc.

4. **Failover Strategies and Recovery Procedures**:

In case of server failure, the system should switch to a backup system. This is typically achieved by running multiple replicas of your servers and using health checks and heartbeats to detect failures. A common practice here is to use automated rollout and rollback processes for releasing changes in the systems with minimal impact on the running systems.

5. **Monitoring**:

Continuous system monitoring helps to ensure system availability. Building real-time monitoring and alerting into the system allows for prompt reaction when issues occur. This could include tools for log management and system metrics.

Hence, A sample architecture diagram for the system can be as follows:

```
graph TB
  A[Internet] -- SMTP/Data --> B[Load Balancer]
  B -- SMTP/Data --> C[Server 1]
  B -- SMTP/Data --> D[Server 2]
  C -- Sync --> D
  D -- Sync --> C
  C -- Write --> E[Database 1]
  D -- Write --> F[Database 2]
  E -- Replicate --> F
  F -- Replicate --> E
```

In all, designing an email delivery system for high availability requires ensuring that the infrastructure can handle high traffic and is not prone to single points of failure by deploying several strategies including redundant and distributed systems, load balancing, data replication, regular health checks, and robust monitoring and alerting systems.

12.6 How would you design a service to monitor the uptime of a million websites?

Designing a service to monitor the uptime of a million websites can be a challenging task considering the scale and reliability required. Here are some steps:

1. **Divide & Conquer**: We are tackling a huge number of websites (a million!). Hence, we need to divide the tasks into manageable chunks. Allocate a fixed number of websites to each worker server and make sure no two servers are checking the same website.

2. **Fault Tolerance**: Every system can fail, hence, it's important to design a fault-tolerant system. If one worker server dies another should take over its job.

3. **Choosing an Efficient Data Structure**: We can use a HashMap where key is URL and value is a boolean array of size 24*60 (n). This boolean array will represent the status of each minute of the last 24 hours. 1 indicates up and 0 indicates down.

4. **Notifications**: Users should be notified when any tracked website goes down or comes back up. An observer pattern should be incorporated into the system.

5. **Selected Websites Balancing**: Put the monitored websites into a database, distribute cases to various servers according to the workload and remain flexible to the server performance.

Let's look more in detail about these points.

Multithreading

Given the huge number of websites, we can use multiple threads on each server. Each thread is responsible for checking the status of one or more websites. This way, we can monitor more websites simultaneously.

```
import requests

def is_site_alive(url):
    response = requests.head(url)
    return response.status_code == 200
```

Fault tolerance

For ensuring this, we can maintain a master server, which is responsible for distributing the load among the worker servers. Master server will continuously monitor the heartbeat of worker servers. If any server dies, the master server can reallocate the websites to other servers.

Choosing an Efficient Data Structure We need to query the status of the site for the last 24 hours. These are 24 * 60 = 1440 minutes. Hence, for quick retrieval and updates, we can keep them in main memory.

```
class WebSite:
  def __init__(self):
    self.status = [False] * (24 * 60) # Initialize with False

  def update(self, minute, is_alive): # O(1) operation
    self.status[minute] = is_alive

  def status_last_day(self): # O(1) operation
    return self.status
```

Notifications

Observer pattern can be used to notify users. Websites are 'subjects' and users are 'observers'. We maintain a list of observers for each subject. When the state of subject changes, all its observers are notified.

Selected Websites Balancing

We use master-slave mode. The master server detects and distributes new tasks, and each slave server automatically reports the running state and receives new tasks. For example, a slave server can monitor 10,000 websites, so we use about 100 slave servers. Alternatively, a load balancer can be put in place to redirect requests to less busy servers, providing a balanced workflow.

In conclusion, system design can considerably vary depending upon the functional and non-functional requirements. The design decisions mentioned above are a good starting point, but each system may require additional optimizations on case-by-case basis.

12.7 Can you design a hotel reservation system?

Designing a hotel reservation system is a common project in software engineering. Here's a simple overview of what such a system might look like.

The system should be capable of managing room bookings for a hotel, which involves keeping track of which rooms are booked, managing room rates, and dealing with customer reservations, cancellations, and associated payments.

Overall, the system would have three major components:

1. User Interface: This component will interact with the users of the system, allowing them to make, update, or cancel reservations, select room types, and make payments.

2. Reservation Management: This component handles the backend logic and databases to keep track of the room inventory, room rates, and reservation records.

3. Payment Processing: This component will manage the financial transactions for the system.

The data we might want to store in this system includes:

- Customer information: Name, contact info, payment details

- Room details: Room type, room cost, room status (Booked/Available)

- Booking details: Booking date, check-in and check-out dates, room type

Here's a high-level Entity-Relationship (ER) diagram for your system:

```
Customer(CustomerId, CustomerName, CustomerContact, PaymentDetails)
Booking(BookingId, CustomerId, CheckInDate, CheckOutDate, RoomType)
Room(RoomId, RoomType, RoomCost, RoomStatus)
```

Note: 'CustomerId' in Booking refers to 'CustomerId' in Customer and signifies a foreign key.

A SQL table creation script for these entities might look as follows:

```
CREATE TABLE Customers (
    id INT PRIMARY KEY,
    name VARCHAR(100),
    contact VARCHAR(100),
    payment_details VARCHAR(100)
);

CREATE TABLE Rooms (
    id INT PRIMARY KEY,
    type VARCHAR(100),
    cost FLOAT,
    status VARCHAR(10)
);

CREATE TABLE Bookings (
    id INT PRIMARY KEY,
    customer_id INT,
    check_in_date DATE,
    check_out_date DATE,
    room_type VARCHAR(100),
    FOREIGN KEY (customer_id) REFERENCES Customers(id)
);
```

You can encapsulate the business logic in application services. For example, to create a reservation, your service might:

1. Query the 'Rooms' table to find an available room on the requested dates.

2. If a room is available, create a record in the 'Bookings' table.

3. Update the status of the room in the 'Rooms' table to 'Booked'.

Overall, to design a more advanced system, you might need to handle edge cases and additional features like handling room maintenance status, room upgrades, booking multiple rooms, group reservations, etc.

In terms of system architecture, this could be a classic 3-tier system:

1. Presentation Layer: This is where your UI lives.

2. Application Layer: This executes the associated application/business logic.

3. Data Layer: This is where data gets stored and retrieved from.

This is certainly a very high-level overview, and there are many details much dependent on the specific needs and scope of the system.

12.8   How would you design a job scheduler for a distributed system?

Designing a job scheduler for a distributed system requires careful consideration of various factors such as job priority, resource availability, and system load. Here is an approach to design a job scheduler for distributed systems:

1. **Job Classification:** Understanding the nature of the job

is the first step in designing job scheduler. Jobs could be CPU-bound, memory-bound, I/O-bound etc. Consider the priority of the jobs, whether they can be executed in parallel, or they have dependencies.

2. **Resource Awareness:** The scheduler should be aware of the resources of the system - how many nodes are there, what is the capacity of each node in terms of CPU, memory, storage, network bandwidth.

3. **Load Balancing:** The scheduler needs to distribute jobs to ensure that all worker nodes have approximately equal workload. It requires keeping track of the number of executing jobs on each node, their resource consumption, and the node-capacity.

4. **Fault Tolerance:** The scheduler should be able to handle failures. If a node fails, the jobs running on that node should be rescheduled to run on some other node.

5. **Data Locality:** In data-intensive jobs, data locality plays a significant role in improving performance. Scheduler should schedule jobs where data is located to reduce data movement over the network.

6. **Scheduling Algorithms:** Various job scheduling algorithms can be used based on the requirements. For instance, First Come First Serve (FCFS), Shortest Job Next (SJN), Round Robin (RR), Priority Scheduling, Fair Sharing etc.

A simple design of job scheduler would have the following components in its architecture:

1. **Job Queue:** It is used to store the incoming jobs to be scheduled for execution. This can be a priority queue for

supporting priority-based job scheduling.

2. **Scheduler:** It takes into account the priorities, dependencies, and resources required for the job. Based on these factors and the scheduling algorithm, it decides which job to assign to which worker node.

3. **Worker Nodes:** They execute the jobs received from the scheduler. They also update the scheduler about their available resources and current load.

Example: In hadoop's MapReduce, YARN (Yet Another Resource Negotiator) acts as a scheduler. The Resource Manager is the main authority that arbitrates resources among all the applications in the system. Node Manager is the per-machine framework agent who is responsible for containers, monitoring their resource usage and reporting the same to the Resource Manager/Scheduler.

Here's a visual representation:

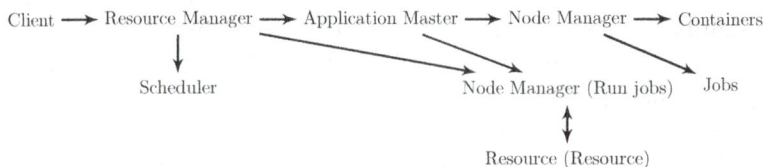

Client ⟶ Resource Manager ⟶ Application Master ⟶ Node Manager ⟶ Containers

Scheduler ⟶ Node Manager (Run jobs)   Jobs

Resource (Resource)

Node manager reports to Resource Manager about resource availability. Resource Manager's responsibility is to allocate resources to different applications based on requirement and priority. Application Master is responsible for accepting job-submissions, negotiating the first container for executing the application specific ApplicationMaster and provides the service for restarting the ApplicationMaster container on failure.

The challenges in such a design include dealing with "starvation" where a low-priority job may never get scheduled if high-priority jobs keep coming. These can be mitigated using techniques like aging, where a job increases its priority if it waits too long in the queue.

12.9 How would you design a distributed lock for a distributed system?

Designing a distributed lock for a distributed system is a complex process that involves making a number of key decisions. Here's a high-level breakdown of how one might design such a system.

1. **Centralized Lock Manager**:

We could create a centralized lock manager that all nodes in the system communicate with to acquire and release locks. This simple approach works well in many cases and has a number of advantages. For example, it's easy to understand and implement, and it guarantees that only one process will be able to acquire a lock at any given time.

However, it also has a number of key drawbacks. For one, it can become a bottleneck, especially in high-throughput systems. Additionally, this design offers a single point of failure.

2. **Distributed Lock Manager**:

On the other hand, we can use a distributed lock manager that either uses a leader-follower design (also known as master-slave) or consensus algorithms like Raft or Paxos to manage locks in a distributed way.

In the leader-follower design, the leader would be in charge of managing lock requests and releasing them. If the leader fails, one of the followers can be promoted to be the new leader.

In contrast, with Paxos or Raft, there is no one leader. Instead, a majority of nodes must agree on granting a lock. This is a more complex solution, but it's also more robust and can better handle failures.

Considerations for either approach include network partitions and node failures. For example, in a network partition, you should prefer availability over consistency (so your system is still accessible), or vice versa (so your system remains consistent), depending upon the requirements.

Here is a pseudo-code example of a simple 'Lock' class that can be used in distributed systems:

```
class Lock:
    def __init__(self):
        self._locked = False

    def acquire(self):
        if not self._locked:
            self._locked = True
        else:
            # handle the lock already being acquired

    def release(self):
        if self._locked:
            self._locked = False
        else:
            # handle the lock already being released
```

In a real-world scenario, you'd probably use Apache Zookeeper or etcd for distributed lock management. In these systems, ephemeral nodes are created when a lock is required. Each node gets a unique ID, and the one with the lowest ID gets the lock. When the lock is released, the node is deleted. This design represents a Leader election process.

For availability of the lock in spite of node failures, use Apache Zookeeper's ephemeral znodes. Zookeeper nodes create a unique znode when they attempt to grab the lock. If the node dies, the znode is automatically deleted.

Please note that distributed locks can have complexities and different conditions to handle problems (like deadlocks etc.). It should be used judiciously and only when it's absolutely required.

The detailed design and implementation for a specific system could vary based on the precise requirements, semantics (like read/write lock) and the technologies in use.

12.10 Can you design a garbage collection system?

Designing a garbage collection system is quite a complex task as it involves understanding memory management and the interaction between the garbage collector and the rest of the software system. To keep this answer at a high level, I'll avoid any specific programming language intricacies and instead focus on the general principles.

A basic garbage collector could be implemented using reference counting or tracing.

1. **Reference Counting Garbage Collector Design:**

In reference counting, every object has a count of the number of references to it. The count is increased every time a reference to an object is made and decreased when a reference to the object is removed. When the count reaches zero, the object is unreachable and is thus considered "garbage" and can be safely deallocated.

Although reference counting is simple and ensures prompt collection of garbage, it has several drawbacks. It does not handle cyclic references well, i.e., two objects referring to each other but not being referenced by any other object. These objects will not be considered garbage even though they may be unreachable from root references.

Here is a simple algorithms representation of reference counting:

```
class Object {
    int count; // Reference count
    Object[] references; // Array of references to other objects
}

function incrementCount(Object o) {
    o.count = o.count + 1;
}

function decrementCount(Object o) {
    if (o.count > 0) {
        o.count = o.count - 1;
    } else {
        // do nothing
    }
}

function collectGarbage(Object[] objects) {
    for each o in objects {
        if (o.count == 0) {
            // This object is garbage.
            // Recursively decrement the reference count of all
                referred objects.
            for each ref in o.references {
                decrementCount(ref);
            }
            // finally de-allocate (delete) object
            delete o;
        }
    }
}
```

2. **Tracing Garbage Collector Design:**

Tracing GCs operate by tracing the graph of object references starting from "root" references, typically including global variables and active call stack variables. Any object that is not found during this trace is unreachable, and therefore considered garbage.

The most typical form of tracing garbage collector is the Mark-and-Sweep GC.

Mark Phase: Starting from root references, traverse the entire object graph. Every object found is marked as being alive.

Sweep Phase: After the mark phase, the collector traverses all objects and reclaims any that are not marked as alive.

Here is a simple algorithms representation for Mark-and-sweep:

```
class Object {
    bool marked; // Mark flag
    Object[] references; // Array of references to other objects
}

function mark(Object o) {
    if (!o.marked) {
        o.marked = true;
        for each ref in o.references {
            mark(ref); // Recursively mark all referred objects
        }
    }
}

function collectGarbage(Object[] objects, Object[] roots) {
    // Unmark all objects
    for each o in objects {
        o.marked = false;
    }
    // Mark all reachable objects
    for each root in roots {
        mark(root);
    }
    // Collect all unmarked objects
    for each o in objects {
```

```
    if (!o.marked) {
        // This object is garbage
        delete o;
    }
  }
}
```

The main drawback with this approach is that during the mark-
and-sweep phase, the application has to be paused to prevent
it from changing the object graph while the garbage collector is
tracing it. This pause can have significant performance implications.

In practice, most modern garbage collectors, like the ones used
in Java and .NET, use a combination of reference counting,
tracing, generational and concurrent collection to balance memory usage, throughput, and pause times. The actual algorithms
used can get quite complicated, but the basic principles are similar to the two designs outlined above.

Afterword

As you find yourself at the end of this book, "Ace the Coding Interview: Must-know Questions," it is my earnest hope that you feel well-equipped, empowered, and prepared for the next steps of your professional journey. This book's pages were designed to give you a thorough grounding in essential software engineering principles and arm you with the know-how and confidence to excel in your technical interviews.

The world of computer science is dynamic and always evolving, so your journey as a developer or engineer does not stop here. Learning in this field is a continuous process, and this book, hopefully, has offered you a solid foundation upon which to continue building your expertise.

In this book, we've covered a wide range of topics, from data structures and algorithms to system design and advanced concepts in distributed computing. Each of these components has its unique importance in the grand scheme of software engineering and hence, the technical interviews that stand as gateways to opportunities in this field.

The breadth and depth of knowledge, the logical reasoning,

and problem-solving abilities you have honed in this journey are not just for acing interviews; they are vital tools you will call upon throughout your career. Remember, the ultimate aim is not to memorize the solutions presented in this book but to understand the principles, patterns, and strategies that guide their construction. It is these understandings that will enable you to tackle new, unfamiliar problems with skill and confidence.

As you move forward, I encourage you to continue challenging yourself. Try solving new problems, read about emerging technologies and trends, work on diverse projects, and learn from your peers and mentors in the field. Always keep the spirit of curiosity and learning alive because that is the heart and soul of any successful career in technology.

While this book marks the end of one chapter in your journey, it also heralds the beginning of another. As you embark on this new chapter, filled with technical interviews and exciting job opportunities, I want you to remember that every challenge you encounter is a stepping stone towards growth and development.

I am grateful for the opportunity to have accompanied you on this leg of your journey. As you close this book, know that you are not just more prepared for your upcoming interviews, but you are also a more knowledgeable and skilled professional. You are ready to face new challenges, create innovative solutions, and make your unique mark in the world of technology.

Here's to your ongoing journey of learning, growth, and success!

Made in the USA
Monee, IL
08 January 2025

76352766R00154